THE FATHERS
OF THE CHURCH

A NEW TRANSLATION

VOLUME 75

THE FATHERS OF THE CHURCH

A NEW TRANSLATION

EDITORIAL BOARD

Thomas P. Halton
The Catholic University of America
Editorial Director

M. Josephine Brennan, I.H.M.
Marywood College

Elizabeth Clark
Duke University

Hermigild Dressler, O.F.M.
Quincy College

Robert B. Eno, S.S.
The Catholic University of America

Daniel J. Sheerin
University of Notre Dame

Robert D. Sider
Dickinson College

Michael Slusser
College of St. Thomas

David J. McGonagle
Director
The Catholic University of America Press

FORMER EDITORIAL DIRECTORS

Ludwig Schopp, Roy J. Deferrari, Bernard M. Peebles,
Hermigild Dressler, O.F.M.

Cindy Kahn
Staff Editor

SAINT GREGORY OF NAZIANZUS

THREE POEMS

CONCERNING HIS OWN AFFAIRS
CONCERNING HIMSELF AND THE BISHOPS
CONCERNING HIS OWN LIFE

Translated by
DENIS MOLAISE MEEHAN, O.S.B.

St. Andrew's Priory
Valyermo, California

Supplementary Notes by
THOMAS P. HALTON

THE CATHOLIC UNIVERSITY OF AMERICA PRESS
Washington, D.C.

Nihil Obstat: Rev. Michael Slusser, S.T.B., D.Phil.
Censor Deputatus

Imprimatur:
Rev. Msgr. Raymond Boland
Vicar General for the Archdiocese of Washington

March 17, 1986

Copyright©1987
The Catholic University of America Press
All rights reserved
Reprinted 1992
First short-run reprint 2001

LIBRARY OF CONGRESS CATALOGING-IN-PUBLICATION DATA
Gregory, of Nazianzus, Saint.
   Three poems.

   (Fathers of the church ; v. 75)
   Translation from the Greek.
   Bibliography: p.
   Contents: Concerning his own affairs — Concerning himself and the bishops — Concerning his own life.
   1. Gregory, of Nazianzus, Saint.   2. Cappadocian Fathers—Biography.   3. Council of Constantinople (1st : 381) Poetry.   I. Title.   II. Series.
BR60.F3G68   [BR1720.G7]   270 s [270'.2'0924]   86-6821
ISBN 0-8132-0075-X
ISBN 0-8132-1305-3 (pbk)
ISBN-13: 978-0-8132-1305-7 (pbk)

CONTENTS

Select Bibliography vii
Abbreviations xi

Introduction 1
I Concerning His Own Affairs 23
II Concerning Himself and
   the Bishops 47
III Concerning His Own Life 75

Index 133

SELECT BIBLIOGRAPHY

Ackerman, W. *Die Didaktische Poesie des Gregorius von Nazianz.* Leipzig 1903
Althaus, H. *Die Heilslehre des heiligen Gregor von Nazianz.* Münster 1972.
*Anthologia Palatina. The Epigrams of Saint Gregory the Theologian. (lib.*8). Edited by W. R. Paton. Loeb. 5 vols. Cambridge, Ma., 1970. 2: 399–505.
Benoît, A. *Saint Grégoire de Nazianze.* Marseilles 1876. Reprint. Hildesheim 1973.
Bernardi, J. *La Prédication Des Pères Cappadociens.* Publications de la Faculté des Lettres et Sciences humaines de L'Université de Montpellier XXX. Paris 1968.
Boulenger, F. *Grégoire de Nazianze. Discours funèbres en l'honneur de son Frère Césaire et de Basile de Césarée.* Paris 1908.
Boyd, H. S. *Select Poems of Synesius and Gregory Nazianzen.* London 1814.
Capes, W. W. *University Life in Ancient Athens.* New York 1877.
Cataudella, Q. "Le poesie di Gregorio Nazianzeno." *Athene e Roma* 8 (1927): 88–96.
Cummings, J. T. "St. Gregory of Nazianzus." *NCE* 6.164–173.
Gallay, P. *La Vie de S. Grégoire de Nazianze.* Paris 1943.
——— and M. Jourjon, eds. *Grégoire de Nazianze. Discours 27–31 (Discours théologique.)* SC 250. Paris 1978.
Geerard, M. *Clavis Patrum Graecorum.* Vol. 2: 3010–3125, esp. 3034–3037. Brepols-Turnhout 1974.
Hauser-Meury, M.-Madeleine. *Prosopographie zu den Schriften Gregor von Nazianz.* Bonn 1960.
Jones, A. H. M., J. R. Martindale and J. Morris. *The Prosopography of the Later Roman Empire.* Vol. 1. Cambridge 1971.
Jungck, Christoph, ed. *Gregor von Nazianz. De vita sua.* Heidelberg 1974.
Kennedy, G. *Greek Rhetoric Under Christian Emperors.* Princeton 1983.
Kertsch, M. *Bildersprache bei Gregor von Nazianz. Ein Beitrag zur spatantiken Rhetorik und Popularphilosophie.* Graz 1978.
———. "Ein bildhafter Vergleich bei Seneca, Themistios, Gregor

von Nazianz und sein kynisch-stoischer Hintergrund." *VigC* 30 (1976): 241–257.
Keydell, R. "Die litterarhistorische Stellung der Gedichte Gregors von Nazianz." *Atti dello VIII Congresso Internazionale di Studi Byzantini*. Vol. 1. Rome 1953: 43–173.
———. "Die Unechteit der Gregor von Nazianz zugeschriebenen *Exhortatio ad virgines.*" *ByZ* 43(1950): 334–337.
———. "Ein dogmatisches Lehrdicht Gregors von Nazianz." Ibid. 44 (1951): 315–321.
Knecht, A., trans. *Gregor von Nazianz: Gegen die Putzsucht der Frauen*. Heidelberg 1972.
Lorenz, B. "Zur Seefahrt des Lebens in den Gedichten des Gregor von Nazianz." *VigC* 33 (1979): 234–241.
Mathieu, J. M. "Remarques sur l'anthropologie philosophique de Grégoire de Nazianze (*Poem. dog.* VIII.22–32, 78–96) et Porphyre." *StPatr* XVII, 3. Edited by E. A. Livingstone. Oxford 1982: 1115–1119.
Meehan, D. "St. Gregory Nazianzen and Hellenic Humanism." *Irish Ecclesiastical Record* 57 (1944): 255–264.
———. "Editions of Saint Gregory of Nazianzus." *Irish Theological Quarterly* 3 (1951): 203–219.
Misch, G. A. *A History of Autobiography in Antiquity*. Vol. 2. London 1951. Pp. 600–624.
Moreschini, C. "Luce e purificazione nella dottrina di Gregor Nazianz." *Augustinianum* 3 (1973): 535–549.
Mossay, J. "Gregor von Nazianz." *TRE* 14 (1985): 164–173.
———. ed. *II.Symposium Nazianzenum (Louvain-la-Neuve, 25–28 août 1981): Actes du colloque international organise avec le soutien du Fonds National belge et de a Recherche Scientifique et de a Gorres-Gesellschaft zur Plege der Wissenschaft*. Studien zur Geschichte und Kultur des Altertums. Neue Folge. 2. Reihe. *Forschungen zu Gregor von Nazianz*. Paderborn 1983.
———. "Perspectives eschatologiques de saint Grégoire de Nazianze." *Questions Liturgiques et Paroissiales* 45 (1964): 320–339.
———. "Gregoire de Nazianzus. Trauvaux et projets recents. Chronique." *Antike und Christentum* 46 (1977): 594–602.
Musurillo, H. "The Poetry of Gregory of Nazianzus." *Thought* 45 (1970): 45–55.
Newman, J. H. *Historical Sketches*. Vol. 2. London 1894. Pp. 55–72.
Norris, F. W. "Of Thorns and Roses. The Logic of Belief in Gregory Nazianzen." *ChH* 53 (1984): 455–464.
Otis, B. "The Throne and the Mountain. An Essay on St. Gregory Nazianzus." *CJ* 56 (1961): 146–165.
Pellegrino, M. *La poesia di Gregorio Nazianzeno*. Milano 1932.

Plagnieux, J. *Saint Grégoire de Nazianze théologien.* Paris 1951.
———. "Saint Grégoire de Nazianze." *Théologie de la vie Monastique.* Études Publiées sous la Direction de la Faculté de Théologie S. J. De Lyon-Fourvière 49 (Aubier 1961): 115–130.
Puech, A. *Histoire de la littérature grecque chrétienne jusqu' à la fin du 4ᵉ siècle.* Vol. 3. Paris 1930. Pp. 310–395.
Quasten, J. *Patrology* 3: *The Golden Age of Greek Patristic Literature from the Council of Nicaea to the Council of Chalcedon.* Utrecht 1960.
Quéré, F. "Réflexions de Grégoire de Nazianze sur la parure féminine. Étude du poeme sur la coquetterie, 1,2,29." *RevSR* 42 (1968): 62–71.
Reuther, R. R. *Gregory of Nazianzus: Rhetor and Philosopher.* Oxford 1969.
Ritter, A. M. *Das Konzil von Konstantinopel und Sein Symbol: Studien zur Geschichte und Theologie des II Oekumenische Konzils.* Forschungen zur Kirchen und Dogmengeschichte 15. Göttingen 1965.
Rousse, J. "Grégoire de Nazianze (saint)." *DSp* 6 (1965): 932–971.
———. "Les anges et leur ministère selon saint Grégoire de Nazianze." *Mélanges de Science Religieuse* 22 (1965): 133–152.
Rudasso, P. R. *La figura di Cristo in S. Gregorio Nazianzeno.* Rome 1968.
Sicherl, M., J. Mossay, and G. Lafontaine. "Trauvaux préparatoires pour une édition critique de Grégoire de Nazianze." *RHE* 74 (1979): 632–635.
Špidlík, T. *Grégoire de Nazianze. Introduction à l'étude de sa doctrine spirituelle.* Rome 1971.
Sykes, D. A. "The Poemata Arcana of St. Gregory Nazianzen." *JThS* XXI (1970): 32–42.
———. "The Bible and Greek Classics in Gregory Nazianzen's Verse." *StPatr* XVII,3. Edited by E. A. Livingstone. Oxford 1982: 1127–1130.
Szymusiak-Affholder, C.-Marie. "Psychologie et Histoire dans le Rêve Initial de Grégoire le Théologien." *Philologus* 115 (1971): 302–310.
Trisoglio, F. "La poesia della Trinita nell' opera litteraria di san Gregorio di Nazianzeno." In *Forma Futuri: Studi in onere del Cardinale Michele Pellegrino.* Torino 1975. Pp. 712–740.
———. "Reminiscenze e consonanze classiche nella XIV orazione di Gregorio di Nazianzeno." *Atti dell' (ar.) accademia delle Scienze in Torino* 99 (1964–1965): 129–204.
Ullman, C. *Gregor von Nazianz der Theologe.* 2d ed. Gotha 1867.
Wagner, M. *Rufinus the Translator: A Study of His Theory and Practice as Illustrated in His Version of the "Apologetica" of St. Gregory Nazianzen.* The Catholic University of America Patristic Studies 73. Washington, D.C. 1945.

Werhahn, H. M. *Gregorii Nazianzi* Σύγκρισις βίων. Weisbaden 1953.
Wyss, B. "Gregor II(Gregor von Nazianz)." *RAC* 12(1983): 793–863, esp. 839–859.
———. "Gregor von Nazianz. Ein griechisch-christlicher Dichter des 4 Jahrhunderts." *Museum Helveticum* 6 (1949): 177–210.

ABBREVIATIONS

Abbreviations of classical texts are from the *Oxford Classical Dictionary*, edited by N. G. L. Hammond and H. H. Scullard. 2d edition. Oxford 1970.
The Latin titles of the works of Saint Gregory of Nazianzus are from the *Thesaurus Linguae Graecae: Canon of Greek Authors and Works*, edited by L. Berkowitz and K. A. Squitiers. 2d edition. Oxford 1986.

SERIES PUBLICATIONS

AnBoll Analecta Bollandiana. Brussels 1882—.

CSEL Corpus Scriptorum Ecclesiasticorum Latinorum. Vienna 1866—.

CUFr Collections Universités de France. Paris 1920—.

FOTC The Fathers of the Church. Washington, D.C. 1947—.

GCS Griechische Christliche Schriftsteller. Berlin 1897—.

Loeb Loeb Classical Library.

NPNF Nicene and Post Nicene Fathers. Second Series. Reprint 1978.

PG Patrologiae Cursus Completus. Series Graeca. Paris 1857–1866.

SC Sources Chrétiennes. Paris 1942—.

TU Texte und Untersuchungen zur Geschichte der Altchristlichen Literatur. Berlin 1882—.

REFERENCE WORKS AND DICTIONARIES

DACL *Dictionnaire d'Archéologie Chrétienne et Liturgie*. Paris 1903–1953.

DHGE *Dictionnaire d'Histoire et de Géographie Ecclésiastique*. Paris 1912—.

DicBib *Dictionnaire de la Bible*. Paris 1928—.

DSp   Dictionnaire de Spiritualité, Ascétique et Mystique. Paris 1932—.
DThC Dictionnaire de Théologie Catholique. Paris 1903—.
NCE   New Catholic Encyclopedia. New York 1967.
OCD   Oxford Classical Dictionary. 2d edition. Oxford 1970.
PGL   Patristic Greek Lexicon. Edited by G. W. H. Lampe. Oxford 1961–1968.
RAC   Reallexikon für Antike und Christentum. Stuttgart 1950—.
TRE   Theologische Realenzyklopädie. Berlin 1974—.

JOURNALS

BySl   Byzantinoslavica
ByZ   Byzantinische Zeitschrift
ChH   Church History
CJ   Classical Journal
JGG   Jahresbericht der Görres-Gesellschaft
JThS   Journal of Theological Studies
KPS   Klassisch-Philologische Studien
RevSR Revue des Sciences Religieuses
RHE   Revue d'Histoire Ecclésiastique
ScC   Scuola Cattolica
StPatr Studia Patristica
VigC   Vigiliae Christianae

INTRODUCTION

INTRODUCTION

LIFE

Saint Gregory of Nazianzus[1] was born either at the town of Nazianzus, or at Arianzus, a country estate bordering the town, in south western Cappadocia, in the year 329 or 330. The estate, according to the usual pattern of Roman provincial *latifundia*, was probably fairly considerable. Fifty years later it was still in the hands of the family.[2] It was here that

---

1. For detailed bibliography of studies on Gregory, cf. Johannes Quasten, *Patrology* 3 (Utrecht 1960): 236–254. See also: Enzo Bellini, "Bibliografia su san Gregorio Nazianzo," *ScCSuppl. bibliografico* 98 (1971): 165–181, J. T. Cummings, "St. Gregory of Nazianzus," *NCE* 6.791–794, J. Mossay, "Gregor von Nazianz," *TRE* 14.164–173, Id., ed., *II.Symposium Nazianzenum (Louvain-la-Neuve, 25–28 août 1981)*, Studien zur Geschichte und Kultur des Altertums, N.S. 2, Reihe, *Forschungen zu Gregor von Nazianz* (Paderborn 1985), J. Rousse, "Grégoire de Nazianze (saint)," *DSp* 6 (1965): 932–971, Francesco Trisoglio, *San Gregorio di Nazianzo in un quarantennio di studi (1925–1965)* (Turin 1970) = *Rivista lasalliana* 40 (1973), B. Wyss, "Gregor II (Gregor von Nazianz)," *RAC* 12 (1983): 793–863.
   Tillemont, *Mémoires pour servir à l'histoire ecclésiastique des six premiers siècles* IX (Paris 1693–1712): 305–360, 692–731 continues to be useful, especially for chronology.
   Chief sources for biography are Gregory's own writings, above all the recently edited poem *De Vita Sua*, a *Vita* by Gregory Presbyter (PG 35.147–242), and there is a life in Suidas' *Lexicon*, for which see C. U. Crimi, "Due citazioni di Gregorio di Nazianzo nel Lex. Suda," *Siculorum Gymnasium*, Facoltà di Lettere e Filosofía dell' Università 31 (1978): 521–523. See also A. Benoît, *S. Grégoire de Nazianze* (Marseilles 1876, reprint 1973), P. Gallay, *La vie de S. Grégoire de Nazianze* (Paris 1943), J. Plagnieux, *S. Grégoire de Nazianze théologien* (Paris 1951).
   There is no full biography in English. Vol. 1 of C. Ullmann, *Gregor von Nazianz der Theologe* (2d ed. Gotha 1867) was translated by G. V. Cox in 1851. See also: Rosemary Radford-Reuther, *Gregory of Nazianzus: Rhetor and Philosopher* (Oxford 1969), D. F. Winslow, *The Dynamics of Salvation: A Study in Gregory of Nazianzus* (Philadelphia 1979).

2. See A. H. M. Jones, J. R. Martindale and J. Morris, *The Prosopography of the Later Roman Empire* 1 (Cambridge 1971): 403 and stemma 17, 1140. Of great importance is Marie-Madeleine Hauser-Meury, *Prosopographie zu den Schriften Gregor von Nazianz* (Bonn 1960).

1

Gregory came after his retirement from Constantinople, and here that he died in 389 or 390. For most of the illustrious ecclesiastics indeed who had origin in Cappadocia in the fourth century, all the information we possess goes to suggest a rather affluent background. For the first time in Christian history we are enabled to observe the results of some generations of Christian belief, combined with wealth, reasonable tranquility, and cultivated standards.[3] By the end of the third century in this province adherents of the new faith, in many cases doubtless the descendants of apostolic converts, seem to have been fairly numerous, and to have made their influence felt in public life well before the edicts of toleration.

The most striking instance, of course, was the family of Saint Basil. His celebrated grandmother, Saint Macrina the Elder, who probably died soon after Gregory was born, and who had borne witness for Christ in the persecution of Diocletian, was a woman of quite unusual attainments. And other womenfolk in Basil's family and in Gregory's are of a pattern: Basil's mother Emmelia, his sister Saint Macrina the Younger, Gregory's mother Nonna, also the daughter of Christian parents, and his sister Gorgonia. Basil's father achieved much more than local reputation in the prestigious profession of rhetor, and Gregory's father, though not a born Christian, was probably some sort of local magnate as well as being bishop of Nazianzus. He had belonged to the Hypsistarian[4] sect, and was baptized into the Christian faith by Leontius, bishop of Caesarea, in 325. In 330 he became bishop of Nazianzus.

It would be interesting if one could determine precisely the racial composition of this class from which people like Gregory and Basil sprang. For more than six hundred years the area had had a fairly chequered history. From being a regular

---

3. J. Bernardi, "Nouvelles perspectives sur la famille de Grégoire de Nazianze," *VigC* 38 (1984): 352–359. See also, T. Kopeček, "The Social Class of the Cappadocian Fathers," *ChH* 42 (1973): 453–466, Id., "The Cappadocian Fathers and Civic Patriotism," *ChH* 43 (1974): 293–303.

4. A Judaeo-pagan sect. See *Or.* 18, *Funebris in patrem*, PG 35.985–1044, FOTC 22.122(5). See also G. Bareille, "Hypsistariens" *DThC* 7,1.572, Lampe, *PGL* 1468, s.v., "Ὑψιστάριοι" and Jungck's note on 51, p. 153 citing Wyss, *Phyllobolia*, 172.

satrapy under the Persian Empire it had gradually passed into the Seleucid kingdom after the conquest by Alexander. Southern Cappadocia, however, had set up a separatist movement and had become a separate kingdom in 255 B.C. It was substantially this kingdom which eventually, in 17 A.D. under Tiberius, became a Roman province. Territorial boundaries were modified under Vespasian, Trajan and Diocletian; and during Gregory's lifetime a division made by Valens was to have considerable effect upon his career.[5] Nazianzus, the town associated with Gregory's name, had received city rights under the name of Diocaesarea in the middle of the first century A.D., but even as late as the fourth century it can scarcely have been a place of much consequence.

Over all these generations of Roman occupation, and the three centuries of Greek influence which preceded it, one must presume profound changes in population. There was probably some admixture of strictly Roman blood, though not at all so much as in provinces of the west and north. Yet the fact that a native, non-Greek, language was the prevailing tongue here as late as the time of Strabo,[6] and is still not quite extinct at the period we treat of,[7] indicates the persistence of a strong native strain. Allowance should always be made for Iranian elements in the thinking and idiom of Cappadocian writers like Gregory. Furthermore contemporary estimates of Cappadocians, which were not flattering, suggest some foreign flavor. With the Cretans and Cilicians they were classed as the "three dreadful Kappas."[8] Their Greek pronunciation was supposed to be faulty. In the heyday of Rome's power it

---

5. A.D. 371. His appointment to Sasima, *Carmina de seipso*, XI.*De vita sua*, PG 37.1059, vv. 439–446, was the indirect result. See *Ep.* 190, Paul Gallay, ed., *Saint Grégoire de Nazianze: Lettres*, vol. 2 (CUFr 1967), Gerhard May, *Die grossen Kappadokier u. die staatliche Kirchenpolitik v. Valens bis Theodosius* (Darmstadt 1976), Ramon Teja, *Organización economica y social de Capadocia en el siglo IV segun los Padres Capadocios* in Acta Salmanticensia. F. y Letras 78 (Salamanca 1974).

6. Strabo 12.1–2.

7. cf. Basil *De Spiritu Sancto*, 29, SC 17.245–254.

8. C. Ullman, *Gregor von Nazianz*, tran. G. Cox, 14, n.2, R. Janin, "Cappadoce," *DHGE* 11.907–909, H. Leclercq, "Nazianze," *DACL* 12,1.1054–1065.

was fashionable to import them as litter-carriers, doubtless because of their superior height and strength.

It is due principally to Gregory that we have so much information concerning his own family and that of Basil. When one considers it, an unusually large proportion of his writing has to do with domestic things and people. To take but one example, the vivid sketches of womenfolk that have come down to us have a unique importance, because they illumine the social pattern of such Christian circles from a rare angle. It is evident that standards for women were high, that feminine influence in training and education was pervasive. In provincial society of this kind this was probably the very characteristic that mainly distinguished Christian families from their pagan contemporaries. Serenity, a certain cultivation and dignity in daily living, seems to be common to both groups at this time, and to all provinces. At no time in history indeed can greater emphasis have been placed by a rural aristocracy on the pursuits of learning and scholarship. In the case of family relationships, however, Christianity seems to have added new dimensions of affection and tenderness. The austere Roman tradition of *patria potestas* is powerfully modified by feminine influence, and in Gregory at least a new warmth and sincerity of feeling is always breaking through the conventional rhetoric of literary genre.

So it is that the early portions of the long autobiographical poem reveal intense feeling for both his parents. He was just as attached to his younger brother, Caesarius,[9] and to his sister, Gorgonia, who seems to have been somewhat older. Apparently there were no other children; but the indications are that numerous relatives lived in the environs, the most noted being Amphilochius, brother of Nonna. His son, of the same name, Gregory's cousin, became bishop of Iconium, a nearby town.

---

9. On Caesarius see Hauser-Meury, 48–58, *Ep.* 29 and 32, P. Gallay, ed., *Lettres*, vol. 1 (CUFr 1964), *Or.*7, *Funebris in laudem Caesarii fratris oratio*, F. Boulenger, ed., *Grégoire de Nazianze. Discours funèbres en l'honneur de son frère Césaire et de Basile de Césarée* (Paris 1908), PG 35.756–788, Gregory, *Epitaphia* 88–100, *Anth. Pal.* 2: 438–444.

High standards again are indicated by the quality of education to which the young Gregory and his brother were exposed. In such a household, of course, the Christian training of the children from the very earliest age would be undertaken and overseen with meticulous care; Nonna in all probability was the principal influence during tender years. However, we know that the usual pedagogue, or tutor, was engaged quite early also. His name was Carterius[10]; he retained always the affection of Gregory, and may very well have remained his companion right through the period of schooling. Subsequently he became a monk. Of himself Gregory tells us that from the very beginning a "passion for letters" possessed him. He attended school, doubtless the usual school of the *grammaticus*, at Nazianzus, and in due time passed to Caesarea, the provincial capital. Here he met Basil for the first time. Afterwards there was a period of protracted wandering in pursuit of learning: from Cappadocia to Caesarea in Palestine, from there to Alexandria and finally to Athens. When he finally returned to Nazianzus he was, he tells us, in his thirtieth year.

At the end of their schooling in Cappadocian Caesarea, Basil and he parted ways for a time. The former went on to Constantinople to continue his study of rhetoric, while Gregory and his brother chose the Christian school in Palestinian Caesarea. The variation is of interest and is probably to be explained by the stronger ecclesiastical influence in Gregory's home. The two Christian schools of Caesarea and Alexandria derived their prestige from the name of Origen. In the interval however their importance must have diminished somewhat, and at this time apparently profane learning of a type similar to that dispensed at sophistic centers everywhere formed part of the curriculum. During Gregory's sojourn at Caesarea, Thespesius, a well-known Christian and a sophist, taught there; and Alexandria was celebrated for its medical school. Gregory was probably drawn there by his brother's decision to follow medicine as a career.[11] He himself does not

10. Gregory, *Epitaphia* 142–146, *Anth. Pal.* 2: 463–465.
11. See *Or.* 7, *Funebris in laudem Caesarii fratris oratio*, F. Boulenger, ed.

appear to have liked Alexandria, and he maintained a prejudice against all Egyptians throughout his life. It was the city that had given Arius to the world. Furthermore, Egyptian intrigues and influence were to cause him considerable embarrassment on more than one occasion as patriarch of Constantinople. During his period as student he probably heard the lectures of Didymus the Blind,[12] and he must have often seen the two great Christian celebrities of Egypt, Athanasius and Antony the Hermit.

The center that really determined Gregory's tastes and formation was Athens. He spent ten years there, he tells us, and left it only with the greatest reluctance. There are even indications that he toyed with the notion of exploiting the high academic reputation he gained there and becoming a professional sophist. Of his hazardous voyage from Alexandria we have a graphic description in the autobiographical poem, the *De vita sua* (vv. 121–210). He was about twenty years old, at the height of his powers and enthusiasm as a student, and as yet unbaptized. Soon he was to be joined again by Basil. For a short time also the young prince Julian was a fellow student, and Gregory has left an unforgettable picture of him as he seemed at that time.[13] Gregory and Basil came to dominate the academic scene at Athens and endlessly discussed the aspirations and ideas that were to color both their lives.

The school was exclusively literary, and was at this time the

---

(Paris 1908), PG 35.756–788, M. E. Keenan, "St. Gregory Nazianzus and Early Byzantine Medicine," *Bulletin of the History of Medicine* 9 (1941): 8–30.

12. See H. Pinault, *Le Platonisme de s. Grégoire de Nazianze* (LaRoche-sur-Yon 1925).

13. *Or.* 5.23, *Contra Julianum imperatorem* 2, PG 35.664–720. On Gregory and Julian see P. Athanassiadi-Fowden, *Julian and Hellenism: An Intellectual Biography* (Oxford 1981), J. Bernardi, ed., SC 309 (1983), Id., "Grégoire de Nazianze critique de Julien," *StPatr* XIV,3 (=TU 117) (Berlin 1976): 282–289, G. W. Bowersock, *Julian the Apostate* (Cambridge, Ma. 1978), R. Browning, *The Emperor Julian* (Berkeley 1976), C. Moreschini, "L'opera e la personalita dell'imperatore Guiliano nelle due 'Invectivae' di Gregorio Nazianzo," in *Forma Futuri: Festschrift Michele Pellegrino* (Turin 1975), 416–430, M. Regali, "Intenti programmatici e datazione delle 'Invectivae in Iulianum' di Gregorio Nazianzo," *Cristianesimo nella storia* 1 (1980): 401–410, S. Scicolone, "Aspetti della persecuzione giulianea," *Rivista di Storia della Chiesa in Italia* 33 (1979): 420–434.

proudest possession of the ancient city, because its political and commercial prestige had waned considerably. While information concerning the administration and organization of such schools is rather scanty, in the case of Athens a good deal emerges from the pages of Eunapius and Libanius.[14] Some of the chairs were endowed by the central government, others by city revenues. License to teach was given by a formal diploma of the city council, and this had to be ratified by imperial consent. Imperial endowment of chairs seems to have been begun by the Antonines. Marcus Aurelius in particular is mentioned for his generosity. In the Theodosian Code we find edicts that stipulate that professors be of good character, and Libanius records an expulsion of three professors by the governor of Greece.

There was considerable competition among the professors, and elaborate touting for students. The students came from everywhere in the Greek world, wore distinctive academic *tribons*, and formed cliques and fraternities very often on the basis of nationality. Among sophists the most celebrated during Gregory's sojourn were Prohairesius, an Armenian and a Christian, Diophantes an Arab, and Epiphanes a Syrian. Eunapius tells us that the Cappadocians regularly supported Prohairesius. Doubtless he was Gregory's chief teacher, as well as Basil's.

Some idea of the encyclopedic curriculum at Athens can be gleaned from Gregory's funeral oration on Basil.[15] It embraced grammar, rhetoric, ethical and metaphysical philosophy, dialectic, mathematics, astronomy. Another contempo-

---

14. Cf. W. W. Capes, *University life in Ancient Athens* (New York 1877): 66ff. See also: George A. Kennedy, *Greek Rhetoric Under Christian Emperors* (Princeton 1983) chps. 3 and 4, P. Petit, *Libanius et la vie municipale à Antioche au IV. siècle après J.-C.* (Paris 1956), Socrates, *Hist. Eccl.* 4.26.

15. See *Or.* 43, *Funebris oratio in laudem Basilii Magni Caesareae in Cappadocia episcopi*, PG 36.513–532, FOTC 22.5–25. For a detailed analysis cf. G. Kennedy, *Greek Rhetoric*, 228–237, who characterizes it as "a remarkable speech, probably the greatest piece of Greek rhetoric since the death of Demosthenes." For Gregory's humanism see F. Trisoglio, "La *humanitas* di Gregorio di Nazianzo attraverso ai suoi tre più ampi carmi autobiografici," *ScC* 105 (1977): 567–594, a study based on the three poems translated in the present volume.

rary source, the sophist Himerius, sketching the formation of his friend Hermogenes, speaks of philosophy, physics, and theology which covered the totality of Greek thought. The Latin language and literature appear to have been ignored. Gregory actually mentions his ignorance of the language.

Study of his writings gives evidence of acquaintance with the following formidable list of authors, principally no doubt the fruit of his Athenian years: Homer, Hesiod, Phocylides, Theognis, Simonides, Pindar, Callimachus, Theocritus, Apollonius of Rhodes, Aratus, various other poets of the *Palatine Anthology*, Herodotus, Thucydides, Plutarch, Diogenes Laertius, Lucian, Evagoras, Socrates, Lysias, Demosthenes, Plato, Aristotle, Heraclitus, Philo Judaeus.[16] It is likely, of course, that a great deal of reading was done in anthologies, or private collections of passages for comparison made by individual sophists; but even by contemporary standards Gregory must have been unusually learned.

One very important result of the years at Athens was the elaboration in concert with Basil of some sort of project for monastic life. Discussions concerning the "philosophic life," and tentative experiments, seem to have been fashionable among young Christians at the universities of both east and west throughout the century. We gather that the two talented Cappadocians became noted figures throughout all Greece. Their way of life as students probably had an ascetic pattern which attracted attention. Everywhere the fame of ascetic pioneers in the Egyptian desert was spreading. As we know from the testimony of Jerome and Augustine, it was shortly afterwards to have a tremendous effect as far west as Rome. The indications are that at Athens Gregory and Basil engaged themselves by a definite promise to undertake some form of contemplative life. Subsequent events or subsequent choices

16. E. Fleury, *S. Grégoire de Nazianze et son Temps* (Paris 1930), 76 ff. For Gregory's classical knowledge see especially B. Wyss, "Gregor von Nazianz," *RAC* 12 (1983): 793ff. For Plato see C. Moreschini, "Il platonismo cristiano di Gregorio Nazianzo," *Annali Sc. Norm. Sup. Pisa*, Cl. di lett. e filos 3 (1974): 1374–1392.

frustrated this undertaking, and in Gregory's case at least the disappointment was never altogether healed.

It is not quite certain when exactly he received baptism.[17] For many young Christians it was customary to remain catechumens. Nevertheless on the voyage to Athens he had been so terrified because of his unbaptized state that he may very well have made all haste to remedy the defect. If not at Athens, where the religious life, he tells us, of Basil and himself was so exemplary, he was certainly baptized soon after his return to Nazianzus, about the year 360. Basil had left Athens at an earlier date, and was probably just then engaged upon his tour of monastic sites in the east.

Between Gregory's return to his home and his appointment to the see of Sasima in 371 a period elapsed of at least ten years. One could interpret a brief remark of his as evidence that he practiced for a while as a rhetorician; but the time was mainly spent in assisting his aging father, discussing and living the ascetic life with Basil at the latter's retreat by the river Iris in Pontus, and in ordering domestic affairs. The brief reign of Julian was an anxious time for all Christians, especially the intellectuals among them, and it imposed a particular strain on the bishop's family at Nazianzus. Caesarius, the younger son, was now a physician at Julian's court. His faith seemed to be endangered, and among Gregory's letters is a moving appeal to him to abandon his career and come home.[18] Caesarius did not in fact return, but neither did he abandon Christianity, though the emperor attempted to win him over.

The joint monastic enterprise of Basil and Gregory in Pontus seems to have been carried out intermittently during all these years, until Basil's elevation to the see of Caesarea led to other preoccupations. Gregory could never quite make up his mind; his keen sense of obligation towards aging parents made any definite break with home seem too drastic. Some-

---

17. See D. F. Winslow, "Orthodox Baptism—A Problem for Gregory of Nazianzus," *StPatr* XIV, 3 (=TU 117) (Berlin 1976): 371–374.
18. *Ep.* 7, P. Gallay, ed., *Lettres*, vol. I (1964) = GCS 53 (1969): 8.

times he was in Pontus, sometimes in Nazianzus. In 362, under pressure from his father, he was ordained to the priesthood, and he experienced, as he did on a few subsequent occasions, an extreme nervous recoil from responsibility. The oration *Apologeticus de fuga* was written to explain his reaction. Out of all this decade of debate and experiment there were two lasting achievements: the *Rule of St. Basil,* in which Gregory almost certainly collaborated and which became the basis of the Benedictine Rule and thus of the whole monastic movement, and the *Philokalia Origenis,* a joint anthology made by the two friends from Origen's writings.

In 370 Basil, who by then had probably made several monastic foundations, became bishop of Caesarea, and in 371, when an administrative division of Cappadocia made by Valens threatened to weaken his authority, he persuaded Gregory to become bishop of Sasima. About Gregory's reaction to this and his experience in Sasima the autobiographical poem *De vita sua* leaves us under no illusion. He does not seem to have exercised any normal ministry in the town. As bishop he acted as coadjutor to his aged father, and, after the latter's death in 374,[19] he continued to administer the church of Nazianzus pending the appointment of a legitimate successor. When the bishops concerned showed some reluctance to do this, he again reacted rather dramatically by withdrawing to the monastery of Saint Thecla at Seleucia in Isauria.

Apart from the long retirement at the end of his life the retreat at Seleucia was to give Gregory his most undisturbed years. It was not until 379, after the death of Basil, that overtures were made to him by the orthodox community at Constantinople. For a considerable time, because of imperial support for the Arians, the Nicaean group of Christians had been deprived of all influence and of all ecclesiastical property in the metropolis. With Valens' death, they saw an opportunity of establishing themselves less precariously. They invited Gregory to be their leader and pastor.

From one point of view it was a puzzling selection. Grego-

---

19. See Hauser-Meury, 90, 135.

ry's ecclesiastical career to date was in many ways far from promising, nor was his strictly theological contribution at all considerable as yet. His reputation as an orator, which dated from Athens, must have been his principal qualification as a strong leader at this stage. In the fourth century, if anything could be calculated to bridge theological gulfs and attract attention, whatever the religious environment, it was oratorical brilliance. It is also likely that strong pressure was brought to bear on Gregory, and that only his deep concern for the defense of orthodoxy against the Arians and other heretical groups induced him to accept. In any case the mission to Constantinople was destined to launch him into the very forefront of ecclesiastical affairs for an intense period of two years; and the challenge of heresy was to elicit from him some of the best writing in the field of speculative theology that the century had seen.

His performance really was remarkable. On arrival at the city, he found everything in Arian hands and was forced to use a private dwelling presented by a relative as church and meeting place. He called it, doubtless to symbolize what he hoped to achieve, the church of Anastasia, and throughout his final years seems to have thought of it with affection and nostalgia. Opposition initially was keen, and not apparently confined to heretical groups. On at least one occasion during one of those religious pogroms that were all too frequent, a result of controversy in cities like Constantinople and Alexandria, he was faced with violence. In many asides of the orations and poems one can discern the lines of criticism of his person. Characteristically, the things said were often illogical and contradictory; but they hurt his sensitivities. He was an uncouth provincial untouched by city elegance; his monkish habits made him a misfit as metropolitan prelate; he was naive and easily put upon; he had no experience or talent for administration; he was unsocial and inhospitable; he laid too much stress on doctrine; he was too conciliatory; he was not conciliatory enough.

Withal, before twelve months had elapsed, he had survived initial opposition and consolidated himself in city life as a figure of consequence and respect. Above all he applied himself to proclamation of orthodox Trinitarian doctrine, and the five *Theological Orations* earned him in subsequent Greek tradition the sobriquet that had been that of the apostle John, *theologos*. At the end of 380, when Theodosius made his triumphal entry as emperor to Constantinople, he was formally installed in the Church of the Apostles as patriarch. Of Theodosius he speaks with respect, but with an approval that is rather qualified.

The three main crises of his sojourn in Constantinople, all of which he describes in the autobiographical poem, *De vita sua*, were the episode of Maximus, the recognition of Gregory by Theodosius, and the Council of Constantinople which led to his resignation and retirement. The story of Maximus the Cynic is quite extraordinary. He arrived in the metropolis with the recommendation of the church of Alexandria, ostensibly a Christian convert from the ranks of Cynic philosophers. All the time he continued to affect the Cynic style: long hair, grave mien, doubtless a wallet and staff. Almost immediately he attached himself to the orthodox group, and succeeded in worming himself so thoroughly into Gregory's confidence that the latter actually preached a eulogy on him. Then, by bribing some confederates, including one of Gregory's clerical entourage, he planned to oust Gregory and have himself installed as patriarch. The arrival of the Egyptian fleet gave him further support, and the conspirators were actually in the midst of a consecration ceremony when the alarm was sounded and they were driven from the church by an outraged congregation. In order to conclude the ceremony they were forced to adjourn to the house of a flute player. The result of the whole fracas was simply to reinforce Gregory's popularity; and an attempt by Maximus to interest Theodosius (who was still in Macedonia) in his claims proved completely unsuccessful. Gregory's reaction to the incident was typical. He tried to escape into solitude, but his congregation refused to entertain the idea. It is probable however, and indeed he hints this, that he had to endure a good deal of adverse comment for the manner in which he had been duped by the Cynic impostor.

The recognition by Theodosius was of considerable moment. When the new emperor entered the city on November 21, 380, there must have been a good deal of uncertainty. It seemed likely that he would proceed against the Arians, but on the other hand the prestige of the orthodox group had suffered because of the Maximus episode. Maximus had already approached Theodosius in Macedonia and had been rebuffed. Would Gregory fare any better? At his first interview the situation was clarified. In Gregory's own account Theodosius makes the momentous statement: "God through me is handing over the church to you and to your labors." This would mean the expulsion of Arian incumbents from all churches and church property. In all probability, judging by previous experience, it would mean a general outbreak of violence. Thus Gregory describes in detail the dramatic moment when the Church of the Apostles was invested by imperial troops and he was conducted by the emperor in solemn procession through the city streets into the very sanctuary. He obviously anticipated violent opposition and regards the peaceful transfer as little short of miraculous. The brilliant sunlight that poured into the old basilica at the crucial moment was the finishing touch. Despite the excitement and popular enthusiasm, however, he refused at that moment to occupy the patriarch's throne—"later on there will be a suitable occasion for greater issues."

In the interval between this event and the arrival of the bishops for the council which Theodosius had summoned, Gregory hints that he had ample opportunity to proceed against his opponents had he been so minded. Many others in his place, with imperial force at his disposal, would undoubtedly have pursued that policy. But he decided to be conciliatory. Again, he was probably criticized for this in orthodox circles. He discovered for instance, he tells us, irregularities in the church finances, but chose to ignore the matter for fear religion should be discredited by public investigation.

The Council, which was convened for the spring of 381, was attended by a representative body of eastern prelates. There does not seem to have been any official delegate of Pope Damasus, though the Macedonian bishops, who were in closer touch with the west, gave the impression of having some sort of mandate. Both they and the Egyptian contingent were late in arriving. Proceedings actually began in May 381 and were initially presided over by Meletius of Antioch. This in itself was a controversial circumstance. For some years the so-called schism of Antioch had been a main bone of contention between east and west. Basil had long ago petitioned Rome and Alexandria to secure recognition for Meletius, but they persisted in supporting his rival Paulinus. Paulinus and the bishops in communion with him did not attend the Council.

In the early stages, before the arrival of the Egyptians and Macedonians, Gregory was recognized as legitimate bishop of Constantinople, and after the death of Meletius he presided at the Council sessions. In an effort to resolve the angry situation at Antioch, though he had been a strong supporter of Meletius and speaks of him in the most affectionate terms, he proposed that no successor be elected. If Paulinus were recognized until his death, time would solve the problem. This eminently sensible proposal however ran counter to the strong antiwestern sentiments of the fathers, and they proceeded to elect Flavian. At this juncture a further crisis was precipitated by the arrival of contingents from Egypt and Macedonia, "a cold wind from the west," is Gregory's vivid phrase.

They seem to have challenged all previous decisions of the Council, and actually questioned Gregory's own position by invoking Canon 15 of the Council of Nicaea, which forbade the translation of a bishop from one see to another. He was, they contended, legitimate bishop of Sasima, not of Constantinople. The combined setbacks were too much for Gregory's sensitivities. He was mortally hurt, made a speech of resignation to the Council, secured the consent of Theodosius, and withdrew once and for all to his boyhood home of Arianzus.

He was privately assured, he tells us, by those concerned, that nothing personal was intended in the questioning of his legitimacy at Constantinople. He does not appear to have been convinced, and he may conceivably have been right. Throughout two poems, which must have been written while he was still smarting from the Council experience, there is a distinct note of acerbity whenever he mentions Egyptians or Macedonians. Some remarks suggest that he suspected opponents of having maneuvered him into resignation, and he accuses Peter, the aged patriarch of Alexandria, of having played a part that was less than straightforward. When all allowance has been made for conventional rhetoric and the satirical style that was the fashion, there does seem to be a residue of animosity against actual persons. In the second poem particularly he speaks with considerable hauteur and contempt of some of the bishops. They are *parvenus*, ill-mannered, ill-educated and turbulent. In general he seems to feel that the standards of piety and cultivation demanded in promoting candidates to this high office are far less than adequate.

From 381 onwards he lived in complete retirement at his home, exercising a distant and benevolent sort of surveillance over his native church of Nazianzus. Most of the letters and poems were written during this period, and it is clear that his interest in church affairs, and his ties with old and highly placed friends remained undiminished. It was probably the happiest period of all his life, when he could devote himself to contemplation undisturbed. He was in touch with various young relatives and his influence and advice were often sought. His articulate championing of orthodoxy in Constantinople placed him on a sort of pedestal, the authority to whom people appealed in order to settle matters of doctrine. His letters concerning the Apollinarian controversy, for instance, are really doctrinal treatises, and were used at the Councils of Ephesus and Chalcedon as classic formulas of

Catholic belief. Nothing, however, would induce him to reconsider his decision about maintaining his retirement, and he steadfastly resisted all the pressure Theodosius brought to bear on him concerning attendance at the Second Council of Constantinople. Right up to the end, which came in 389 or 390,[20] he maintained a long silence, cared for his health which had always been indifferent, and wrote prodigiously, mainly in verse.

WRITINGS

The works of Gregory that have come down to us comprise Orations, Letters and Poems. Outside the pages of Migne a large proportion of this material is still unavailable to readers. Except for the *Theological Orations*, which became so celebrated, Gregory is actually much less theological in content than his great contemporary Basil. Nevertheless, so high was his reputation as scholar and stylist that anything from his pen was viewed with particular reverence, and there is evidence that he continued to be studied for centuries with great intensity.[21] Everything he wrote bears the stamp of the polished rhetorician, his manipulation of figures and cadences being superbly skillful. Much of this is missed in translation. The fairly turgid taste of the time was partial to excess, and Gregory's compositions were in large part designed for declamation on formal and ceremonious occasions.

ORATIONS

The forty-five orations[22], which were probably a selection made after his death, constitute his principal claim to fame in

20. See P. Nautin, "La date du *De viris illustr.* de Jérôme, de la morte de Cyrille de Jérusalem et de celle de Grégoire de Nazianze," *RHE* 56 (1961): 33–35.
21. See J. Noret, "Grégoire de Nazianze, l'auteur le plus cité, après la Bible, dans la littérature ecclésiastique byzantine," J. Mossay, ed., *II.Symposium Nazianzenum*, 259–266. See also A. C. Way in P. O. Kristeller and F. E. Cranz, eds., *Catalogus Translationum et Commentariorum: Medieval and Renaissance Latin Translations and Commentaries* 2 (Washington, D.C. 1971): 43–192.
22. Among recent editions see: *Orationes* 1–3, 4–5, J. Bernardi, ed., SC

the eastern church. Down to the eleventh century they were carefully commented upon and may even have been used as models in the schools of rhetoric. Very shortly after his death nine were translated into Latin, but rather hastily and indifferently, by Rufinus of Aquileia.[23] The forty-five we possess may be roughly classified thus:

(1) Theological. The five *Theological Orations* (27–31)[24] were preached in the church of Anastasia in Constantinople in explanation of the Nicaean doctrine of the Trinity.

(2) Occasional discourses and moral essays. These comprise a great number of which the *Apology for his Flight*,[25] *On his Consecration to Sasima, On the Plague of Hail, On Peace* (three orations), *On Love of the Poor, On Moderation in Theological Discussion*, and the *Farewell Discourse at Constantinople* are the most notable.

(3) Sermons for liturgical feasts.[26] There are two for Easter, one for Christmas, one for Epiphany, one for Low Sunday, one for Pentecost.

(4) Funeral eulogies and panegyrics on saints. He has funeral orations[27] on his father, on Basil, on Caesarius, on Gorgonia; panegyrics on saints Cyprian and Athanasius, and on the Maccabees.

(5) Controversial. The two *Invectives against Julian*,[28] which are quite early and were probably occasioned by Julian's restrictive decree about education, amount to being political pamphlets, particularly virulent in tone.

247/309 (1978/83); 20–26, J. Mossay, ed., SC 270/284 (1980/81); 27–31, P. Gallay, ed., SC 250 (1978). For a general orientation cf. J. Bernardi, "Saint Grégoire de Nazianze" in *La Prédication des Pères Cappadociens*, Deuxieme Partie (Paris 1968), 93–260.

23. For Rufinus see A. Engelbrecht, *Tyranni Rufini orationum Gregorii Nazianzeni novem interpretatio*, CSEL 46 (1910).

24. See P. Gallay, and M. Jourjon, eds., *Grégoire de Nazianze Discours 27–31 (Discours Théologiques)*, SC 250 (Paris 1978).

25. See SC 247.84ff.

26. See J. Mossay, *Les fêtes de Noël et d'Épiphanie d'après les sources littéraires cappadociennes du IVe siècle* (Louvain 1965), esp., 54–59.

27. For funeral eulogies cf. R. C. Gregg, *Consolation Philosophy: Greek and Christian Paideia in Basil and the Two Gregories* (Cambridge, Ma. 1975), 72–74.

28. On Julian see J. Bernardi, ed., *Discours 4–5 contre Julien*, SC 309 (1983), C. Moreschini in *Forma Futuri*, 416–430.

LETTERS

The collection of letters was probably made by Gregory himself originally for the use of his relative Nicobulus. There are 244 letters in the Migne corpus, and an additional one was discovered by Giovanni Mercati. Of the Migne collection three (42, 241 and 243) are not authentic, and some errors with regard to addresses have also crept in.[29] Except for a few which are concerned with doctrinal issues, these tend to be occasional and domestic in tone, and date for the most part from his period of final retirement at Arianzus. But their value is perhaps enhanced for precisely this reason. Light is thrown upon the mundane preoccupations of a man who had been a great public figure, and now numbers all sorts of people—bishops, public officials, rhetors, and of course numerous relatives—among his correspondents. In the fourth century the letter was a distinct literary genre and was practiced as an art by all cultivated people. Gregory's samples are models of conventional form for whatever occasion: letters of recommendation, of reproof, of sympathy, of apology, petitions, invitations and replies to invitations. Invariably they are written with meticulous regard for the canons of style, elaborate Byzantine politesse being a constant feature, together with, as the occasion demands it, touches of humor, gentle irony or parody. It is clear from letters 51 and 54, where he analyzes the theory of epistolary style for Nicobulus,[30] that his own compositions are designed to exemplify the particular style for each occasion as inculcated by the best exponents.

29. On all questions concerning *Epistulae* see P. Gallay, ed. *S. Grégoire de Nazianze. Lettres*, 1 (1–100) (CUFr 1964), 2 (103–201, 203–249) (CUFr 1967). These are united in P. Gallay, ed., *Gregor von Nazianz Briefe*, GCS 53 (Berlin 1969). This critical text of the Letters made a real step forward in the study of Gregory. The history of the text has been singularly unfortunate. Cf. D. Meehan, "Editions of Gregory of Nazianzus," *Irish Theological Quarterly* 3 (1951): 203–219. See also B. Wyss, "Gregor von Nazianz oder Gregor von Nyssa? (Greg. Naz. epist. 249 Gallay/Greg. Nyss. epist. 1 Pasquali)," in *Mémorial André-Jean Festugière: Antiquité païenne et chrétienne* Cahiers d' Orientalisme X (Genève 1984): 153–162.

30. On Nicobulus see G. Dennis, "Gregory of Nazianzus and the Byzantine Letter," in *Diakonia: Studies in Honor of Robert T. Meyer* (Washington, D.C. 1986), 3–13.

POEMS[31]

Three of the longer poems are translated in this volume. His total output in verse, during the last ten years of his life, is little short of prodigious. More than three hundred pieces of varying length, character and quality are extant, in all some nineteen thousand verses in hexameters, trimeters or elegiacs. In Migne they are roughly classified into two books, I Theological Poems and II Historical Poems. Book I is further subdivided into Dogmatic (38 poems) and Moral (40 poems): Book II into poems concerning himself (99 poems) and concerning others (8 poems). Even though the collection exercised a profound influence on the subsequent development of Byzantine hymnology, and we find several of Gregory's epigrams in the *Palatine Anthology*,[32] very few items are really interesting as poetry. It is the autobiographical and topical data that can be assembled from the moral poems of the first book, and from the second book as a whole, which engage the interest of the historian.

31. Work is in progress on a complete critical text. See M. Sicherl, "Bericht über die Entwicklung des Forschungsunternehmens Gregor v. Nazianz," *JGG* 1980 (1981), 121–122, M. Sicherl, J. Mossay, G. Lafontaine, "Travaux préparatoires," *RHE* 74 (1979): 626–640. See also M. Sicherl, "Bericht über die Arbeit an den Gedichten Gregors von Nazianz seit Koblenz" (1976) in J. Mossay, ed., *II.Symposium Nazianzenum*, 137–140. The text tradition of the poems is being systematically published: W. Höllger, *Die handschriftliche Überlieferung der Gedichte Gregors von Nazianz*, mit Vorwort und Beiträgen v. M. Sicherl, und den Übersichtstabellen zur handschriftliche Überlieferung der Gedichte Gregors von Nazianz v. H. M. Werhahn, Studien zur Geschichte und Kultur des Altertums, N.S. 2, *Forschungen zu Gregor von Nazianz*, Vol. 3 (Paderborn 1985). For individual poems in separate editions see: *Carmina moralia* 8 (PG 37.649–667), = *Comparatio vitarum*, Hans Martin Werhahn, ed., *Gregorii Nazianzeni* Σύγκρισις βίων in *KPS* 15 (Wiesbaden 1953); *Carmina moralia* 29 (PG 37.884–908), Andreas Knecht, ed., *Gegen die Putzsucht der Frauen* (Heidelberg 1972); *Carmina de seipso*, XI.*De vita sua* (PG 37.1029–1166), Christoph Jungck, ed., *Gregor von Nazianz. De Vita sua* (Heidelberg 1974); *Carmina quae spectant ad alios* 8 (spurium), E. Oberg, ed., *Amphilochii Iconiensis iambi ad Seleucum* in Patristische Texte und Studien 9 (Berlin 1969). See also A. Tuilier, *Grégoire de Nazianze: La passion du Christ*, SC 149 (Paris 1969): 124–338.

32. In addition to n. 10 *supra* see H. Beckby, ed., *Anthologia Graeca* II Buch VIII *Epitaphien* (München 1957), C. Peri, *Gregorio di Nazianzo Epitaffi* (Milan 1975), P. Waltz, G. Soury *et al.*, eds., *Anthologie Palatine* VIII, *Epigr. 359–827* (CUFr 1944).

Part of Gregory's reason for writing in verse was undoubtedly the provision of some sort of Christian poetic literature,[33] possibly for schools. We have other evidences of this development, especially after Julian's attempt to expel Christians from the schools. And it is clear from the history of the Arian and Apollinarian controversies that versification in the doctrinal field had become quite a fashion. The poem *Concerning His Own Life* is the earliest piece of Christian autobiography we possess, and is in many ways a not unworthy antecedent of Augustine's *Confessions*, which it very probably influenced. Previous autobiographical writing, of which Greek literature provided some examples, was doubtless well known to Gregory;[34] and in particular the idea may have been suggested to him by the autobiographical oration of Libanius the sophist,[35] which had appeared some years previously. It is interesting to note the prominence given by Gregory to details of infancy and childhood. He was the first to do this, and his example was to be followed with signal success by Augustine. The piece *Concerning His Own Affairs*, the first printed in this volume, provides interesting contrast. It was certainly written much earlier, probably about 371. It canvasses many of the personal experiences that were later to be treated again, and is noticeably more Homeric in style. Most of Gregory's compositions indeed, and particularly his poetry, are filled with echoes and imitations from his vast reading;[36] but this piece could be de-

---

33. See D. A. Sykes, "The Bible and Greek Classics in Gregory Nazianzen's Verse," *StPatr* XVII,3 (Oxford 1982): 1127–1130, Id., "The Poemata Arcana of St. Gregory Nazianzus," *ByZ* 72 (1979): 6–15, F. Trisoglio, "La poesia della Trinita nell'opera litteraria di S. Gregorio il Nazianzo," in *Forma Futuri*, 712–740.

34. See G. A. Benrath, "Autobiographie christliche," *TRE* 4.772–777, G. Misch, *A History of Autobiography in Antiquity*. 2 vols. (London 1950), esp., for Gregory, 2:600–624.

35. *Or.* 1, *In sanctum Pascha et in tarditatem* (PG 35.396–401). Cf. A. F. Norman's edition of *Libanius' Autobiography* (Oxford 1965). Comparison of the two works is interesting. The approach to the whole autobiographical theme, selection of incidents and the like, is similar in many ways. Cf. with Gregory Libanius 5 (love of letters); 14 (journey to Athens): 93 (injury to the eye); 118 (earthquake at Nicomedia); 125 (refusal to beg favors from Julian); 275 ff. (trouble with inheritance).

36. On echoes and imitations see *e.g.* B. Wyss, *RAC* 12.835–857.

scribed as a series of variations on Homeric language and techniques.

Concerning Himself and the Bishops, the second poem printed in this volume, is his immediate reaction to experiences at the Council, which is obviously still in session as he writes. In form it is very much a diatribe, where an argument is developed against an imaginary interlocutor. There are very vivid pictures of worldly ecclesiastics. It may even be a little earlier than *Concerning His Own Life*, because Nectarius does not seem to be elected as yet.[37] Both poems must have been written very soon after his return to Arianzus, and their conclusions echo one another. He is still smarting from the humiliation of resignation. The pieces follow somewhat the same pattern, and exhibit the contemporary Hellenistic penchant for *topoi*. We find moralizings about good and evil, about the active and contemplative lives, about inconsistent human behavior, about the nature of eloquence, of friendship, of persuasion, and so on. The exact arrangement of the autobiographical poem, *Concerning His Own Life*, where a few salient incidents only are selected for full description, seems to be due partly to Gregory's apologetic purpose (why he acted as he did at the Council), and partly to certain rhetorical traditions and conventions. On historical, religious, and psychological levels very interesting problems of interpretation arise. Brief portions of this poem have been previously translated by Cardinal Newman in *Verses on Various Occasions* (1888), and by H. S. Boyd, *Select Poems of Synesius and Gregory Nazianzen* (1814). Some of these are reproduced by G. Misch in *A History of Autobiography in Antiquity* (1950). An extensive, but not quite complete, version in French was published by Paul Gallay in 1941. The other pieces have not, to my knowledge, been previously translated.

37. Cf. *Concerning Himself and the Bishops*, n. 62, *infra*.

1 CONCERNING HIS OWN AFFAIRS

De rebus suis II/I/I

(PG 37.969-1017)

OPENING PRAYER, 1–36

O Christ my King. You turned aside the dire might of Amelech, when your servant Moses raised his pure hands after the pattern of the cross in prayer upon the mountain. You fettered the savage jaws of lions and the sharp strength of their claws for Daniel's[1] sake when he stretched out his hands. When Jonas opened wide his arms in prayer within the monster's entrails, he was delivered by your power from the whale.[2] And when the three young men in the Assyrian furnace boldly raised their arms you spread about them a moist cloud. Once, in order to deliver the storm-tossed disciples from the waters, you trod on foot the face of the turbulent deep stilling the waves' and the winds' might.[3] For many a person you have rescued soul and body from disease. You who are God became man and mingled with mortals.

God from all time, you were manifested to us in the fulness of time, so that by becoming man you might make me God.[4] Thus, when I call on you, come as blessed and propitious God. Come to me with helping hand, O my propitious God. Save me, overwhelmed as I am amid war, and wild beasts, and fire, and storm. I have nowhere to turn my gaze except to God alone. All this is brought upon me by evil men, the destroyers of life—wild beasts, the fierce swell of the sea, the horrors of war, the onset of fierce fire. Their chief animosity is directed against people who love God. They do not stand in awe of the coming judgment, and they make of no account the man who hates evil.

---

1. A conflation of biblical figures is very characteristic of Gregory's style. It is really a sophistic technique applied to Holy Writ; cf vv.351–64; 577–695 *infra*. Cf. Ex 17.8–11 (for Amalech and Moses), a text also referred to in *Or.* 12.2, *Ad patrem*, PG 35.845, and Dn 6.23.
2. Cf. Mt 12.40, Jon 2.1.   3. Cf. Mt 14.24–27.
4. On the divinization of man through the Incarnation cf. *Epistulae Theologicae* 101.50, SC 208.58.

From these, O Christ, deliver me. Spread your sheltering wings about me always. O King, drive hateful cares far from your servant. Let not my mind be harassed by grave anxieties, such as this world and the prince of this world devise for hapless mortals. They corrode the godlike image within as rust corrodes iron. The nobler form they reduce to kinship with the earth, so that the soul cannot succeed in elevating the earthbound element of flesh. On the contrary, the flesh drags the winged soul earthwards in misery, enfleshing it in sordid activities.

THE TWO WAYS, 37–62

Among mortals two gates[5] towards hateful death are open. There are those who develop in their mind a turbid spring of evil. They are always concerned with presumptuous deeds, with the body, with wanton satiety, with hateful intrigues. They drive themselves to every transgression, rejoice in evil, love their own doom. The others behold God with the pure eye of the mind. They hate pride which is the shameless offspring of the world. Far from the contaminations of the world they take their course, their flesh wasted to a shadow. Their tread upon the earth is lighter, for they are buoyed up by the Spirit as they follow the God who calls them. Mystics of the hidden life of Christ the King, they go forward in the hope of shining one day for all eternity with the brilliance of that life.

Nevertheless, in the inexorable scheme of things, they are tried by the evil thorns of living. The raging demon, the contriver of evil, devises from without a thousand stings of doom. Alas for mortals in their misery. Worsted in open conflict, the demon often hides hateful destruction under noble guise. He wreaks such havoc against human beings as does the bronze under the bait, which brings destruction to the fish. Seeking

---

5. Cf. Homer, *Il.* 8.15, *Od.* 14.562. For an extended treatment of the two gates by Gregory cf. *Or.* 25.4, *In laudem Heronis philosophi*, SC 284.164 and n.1.

for life they draw the unforeseen bane into their entrails, and
swallow their own doom. So it was with me. After I discovered
the dark character of the evil one, he came at me in fair guise, 60
like unto light. He would have me in my search for light draw
nigh to wickedness, my fickle mind being filched away to its
destruction.

HIS AMBITIONS, 63–101

Marriage, that channel of life, the greatest bond that matter
has forged for human kind, never bound me.[6] The soft weave 65
of silk did not ensnare me. I took no pleasure in the luxuries
of the table, in catering to an insatiable belly which is the wanton mother of lust. Living in great and brilliant houses did
not please me, nor soothing my spirit with the tender strains
of music. I was never surrounded by the soft effeminate scent 70
of myrrh. Others could have their gold and silver: their passion to be surrounded by innumerable possessions brings
them sparse satisfaction and much trouble. Plain fare is my
delight, coarse food I find sweet, and salt and a meagre board,
and with it all a fasting draught of water. Such, with Christ 75
who ever elevates my mind, is my best wealth: no tracts of
fertile land, no fair groves, no herds of kine, no flocks of fat
sheep. Nor yet devoted slaves, my own race who have been
separated from me by an ancient tyranny. To people sprung 80
from one land it gave the double name of freemen and slave.
Nay, not from one land, from one God. And so came into
being this sinful distinction.[7]

Human respect, soon evanescent like the wind, never woke
need in me, nor glory that is doomed to perish. I did not seek 85
to hold high place in the royal court: I was not consumed by

---

6. For Gregory's attitude to virginity and marriage cf. J. Plagnieux, "Saint Grégoire de Nazianze," in *Théologie de la Vie Monastique*, Études Publiées sous la Direction de la Faculté de Théologie S. J. De Lyon-Fourvière 49 (Aubier 1961): 115–130.

7. For the Fall as the cause of slavery cf. J. Weeger and A. Derville, *s.v.*, "Esclave," *DSp* 4,1.1071–1080.

ambition for distinguished seats of justice where I might don haughty airs on a lofty perch. Nor did I covet great influence in the state or among citizens, or take any joy in such vain and feeble dreams, that flutter this way and that and always vanish. Not for me the task of trying to embrace the onrushing river, clasping shadows in my hand, groping after mist. Such are the generations of mortals, such is prosperity, as slight as the wake the ship leaves behind, perceptible for a while but then dissolving into nothing.

The fame that goes with letters was the only thing that absorbed me. East and West combined to procure me that, and Athens, the glory of Greece. I labored much for a long time in the craft of letters; but even these two I laid prostrate before the feet of Christ in subjection to the Word of the great God.[8] It overshadows all the twisted, variegated products of the human mind.

DOMESTIC WORRIES, 102–164

Such dangers then, I managed to avoid. But I did not succeed in avoiding the deceitful hatred of the evil one. He makes ambush under seemingly benevolent guise. To all and sundry I shall candidly relate my mishap because thus one escapes the intrigues of the wily beast. In catering to my parents, who were reduced by hateful age and mourning, I thought, O Christ my King, I was doing something pleasing to you and in accordance with your laws. I was the only remaining child, a dubious hope, the barest flicker from a great lamp that was now no more. It is you who grant sons as helping strength to mortals, who set them like a staff to support trembling limbs. People who honor you above all and over all follow the path of piety and evade the woes of this life by

---

8. Cf. T. Camelot, "Amour des lettres et désir de Dieu chez saint Grégoire de Nazianze: les logoi au service du Logos" in *Littérature et religion: Mélanges offerts au chanoine J. Coppin, Mélanges de Science Religieuse* 23 (Lille 1966): 23–30.

making their cables fast to the anchor of your immutable laws. For them you are the beginning and the end.

My mother had inherited from her ancestors the faith that is pleasing to God. This golden chain[9] she cast about her children, displaying in female form the spirit of a man. Only to such degree did she touch the earth and hold converse with the world as would enable her to elevate all this life to the heavenly level, while she directed her footsteps towards the rarer heights. My father had formerly been a wild olive[10] and lived his life among idols. But when grafted into the stock of the genuine olive, he drew such nourishment from that noble root that he came to overshadow the trees and nourished many people with sweet fruit. Hoary of head and hoary of mind, gentle, sweet of speech, he was another Moses[11] or an Aaron who stood as mediator between mortals and the heavenly God. He brought men into union with the great immortal God by means of the rites and sacrifices we practice, such offerings as are made by a spirit inwardly pure.

With such a father and a mother it were impious to compare anyone else, but I do not hesitate to compare them with each other. In caring for them and sheltering their feeble years I consoled myself with the hope that I was fulfilling the most important duty laid upon us by nature. But how true the saying is that for the wrongdoer the path is strewn with pitfalls.[12] Because the good deed in my case merely gave rise to evil.

Night and day my mind and members are consumed by a host of gnawing anxieties that drag me down from heaven to my mother earth. In the first place, to control servants—what a net of destruction. Harsh masters they always hate, but up-

---

9. For the allegorical "golden chain" cf. B. Wyss, *RAC* 12.826, citing *Or.* 21.6, *In laudem Athanasii*, SC 270.120, and *Or.* 31.28, *De spiritu sancto*, SC 250.332.

10. Cf. Rom 11.17–24. See also *Or.*7.3, *Funebris in laudem Caesarii fratris oratio*, PG 35.757, FOTC 22.6(3).

11. In his *Panegyric on his Father, Or.* 18.14, 24, 29, *Funebris in Patrem* PG 35.996–997, 1013, 1020–1021, FOTC 22.130(14), 137(24), 142(29).

12. cf. Homer, *Il.* 8.14.361.

right ones they shamelessly exploit. The former cannot make
them mild, nor the latter docile: against both they breathe
immoderate venom. Then the administration of property. Always to carry the yoke of Caesar on one's shoulders and have
the harsh rebuke of the collector dinning one's ears.[13] The
taxes which property entails destroy all freedom and bind
your lips with a fetter. Caught in the swirl of the teeming
agora, involved in miserable suits before the seats of magistrates, listening to the clamor and counterclamor of litigants,
getting implicated in knotty twists of law, your lot becomes one
of trouble and conflict. Here the wicked are more successful
than the good, the dispensers of the law being prone to bribery from either side. Any villain at all who has money becomes the best of fellows. Without the help of God no one
can avoid fraud and malpractice in company like that. One
has to flee precipitately letting the rascals have the lot, or have
one's better self sullied by their machinations. People who
come near the evil blast of fire will display the grim evidences
either of the fire or the smoke.

SETTLING CAESARIUS' ESTATE, 165–229

All that I could conceivably have borne. But what I endured
and must still expect to endure since the decease of my
brother[14] was a more agonizing blow. There is little hope of
improvement once the unexpected trouble strikes. While he
lived I enjoyed a reputation second to none, wealth or power
of any kind being foreign to all my aspirations. But when he
died my only legacy was one of trouble and woe. The property he had accumulated was partly swallowed up by the gaping earth when Nicaea collapsed in the earthquake.[15] The rest

13. Cf. Jb 39.7,8. On the tax burden cf. *Or.* 19, *Ad Julianum tributorum exaequatorem*, PG 35.1044–1064, and G. Kennedy, *Greek Rhetoric*, 223.
14. See his *Panegyric on his Brother Caesarius, Or.* 7, *Funebris in laudem Caesarii fratris oratio*, F. Boulenger, ed. (Paris 1908), PG 35.756–788.
15. On the earthquake cf. *Or.* 7.15 *Funebris in laudem Caesarii fratris oratio*, PG 35.773, FOTC 22.16(15), *Epitaphia*, 94, *Anth. Pal.*, 440, St. Basil, *Epistulae*

the evil one delivered as prey into the rapacious hands of
rogues. He himself survived the disaster by taking shelter,
and God in heaven spread a protecting hand over that roof.

Poor Caesarius. There was a time when you shone like the
morning star in the imperial palace,[16] your name revered.
Second to none in wisdom and in gentle courtesy, a host of
powerful friends and companions surrounded you. There
were many people whose fell diseases of the body you alleviated, and in your goodness of heart you came to the rescue
of others in poverty. Now that you are dead, you've become
the prey of jackals. They swarm in from every quarter and
snarl about me, and I have not a single relative to rescue me.
A few indeed profess concern, but it is the concern of enemies. They court you until they get something, and hate you
once they get it. Just as when a lofty oak collapses in a storm,
people from every quarter purloin a branch. Or when the
fence collapses round a great vineyard, it is shamefully pillaged by wayfarers and the wild animal from the woods ravages it with his tusk. The harassment I endure is grievous. I
am unequal to satisfying their demands, or to keeping them
at bay.

Long ago I tore my spirit from the world and mingled it
with the shining spirits of heaven.[17] The lofty mind bore me
far from the flesh, set me in that place, and hid me in the
recesses of the heavenly abode. There the light of the Trinity
shone upon my eyes, a light than which I have known nothing
brighter. It is throned on high and gives off an ineffable and
harmonious radiance, which is the principle of all those
things that time shuts off from heaven.

I died to the world and the world to me, and I am become
a living corpse as devoid of strength as a dreamer. Since that

---

26, "To Caesarius, The Brother of Gregory," R. J. Deferrari, ed., *Saint Basil: The Letters,* Loeb, 4 vols. (New York 1926) 1:155 and n.1.

16. For Caesarius in the imperial palace cf. *Or.* 7, *Funebris in laudem Caesarii fratris oratio,* PG 35.764–772, *Epitaphia* 95–96, *Anth. Pal.,* 440–442, FOTC 22.10–15(8–14).

17. Cf. the results of Gregory's vision of Purity and Chastity in his dream cf. *Carmina de seipso,* XLV.*De animae suae calamitatibus carmen lugubre,* PG 37.1370–71, vv.251–262.

day my life is elsewhere; but I groan under the yoke of the crass flesh, which wise men have called the darkness of the mind.[18]

205 When released from this life and this impeded vision, from men who crawl on earth, wander and make to wander, I greatly long to have a purer vision of the stable things. Then, not as formerly, they will be unadulterated by association with
210 obscure images which can set the vision of the keenest mind astray. With the eye of a mind made pure I shall gaze upon truth itself. But all that is still to be.

Things here below amount to sordid smoke or dust for those who have exchanged this life for the great life, the
215 earthly for the heavenly, the destructible for the stable. Consequently I am set upon by all. They refuse to give way, and rush upon a quarry that is all too easy.

Alas, alas, sad dust of Caesarius. He was wont to ward off all the mob from me, and made it possible for me to evade all
220 distress. Never did another revere a brother as he did: the respect he gave me was what another would give a beloved father. What I lament now is not so much his squandered property: I wanted to have it in common with the poor, being myself but a temporary wanderer here below, and dependent
225 on the bountiful hand of the great donor on high. Nor is it death, that mishap abominated by all mortals which fills with bitterness even the gentle soul. Nor yet my brother himself, the people's idol, whom after his brief span the tomb conceals.

HIS SPIRITUAL WOES, 230-306

230 It is my soul that I lament, as one would mourn a queen, fair, and stately, and sprung from a noble line of kings, that he might see languishing, fast in chains, when enemies have taken her with the spear. They have bound her in harsh slavery, and she bends her sad gaze upon the ground. For such was my fate. In such wise am I stricken to the heart.

---

18. For the "darkness of the mind" cf. 2 Pt 2.4, 7–18. See also *Carmina de seipso* XII.*De se ipso et de episcopis*, PG 37.1170, vv. 51–52.

Folklore has it[19] that when the bitter serpent has sunk his malicious fang into someone, that man will reveal the pestilent sore only to those who have been likewise wounded by the same hateful creature's feverish venom. They alone can appreciate its grevious character. So with me. I shall recount my woe to people united with me by love, or misfortune, or similar pain, because they alone could hear the tale with sympathy. They are capable of insight into the mysteries of a laden heart, who yearn to take upon their shoulders the burden of the cross, who have their portion in the fold of the great King, who love the path of rectitude and treat the fallen with compassion.

As for others, the recital of my woes might well seem ridiculous to them. They are the people whose heart has been touched only superficially by the faith, who have never known in their inmost being the sharp stab of desire for the King. Their abode is here below, their concern only for ephemeral things. Upon this they whet the ready weapon of their tongue against everyone alike, be he good or evil. As for me, I shall not give over my laments until I make good my escape from lamentable evil, and place a padlock on the mad passions of the mind. Satan, the evil one, has thrown open all the doors to them, doors that were fast before, when I was sheltered by the hand of God. In those days evil could not approach me, but it is swift to gain a hold. When a reed comes close to a fierce blaze it catches fire, and the wind sends the flame on high.

DESIRE FOR CONTEMPLATION, 261–306

Would to God I had hidden myself in cliffs, and mountains, and crags, before all this came about. Fleeing this world, this way of life and the anxieties of the flesh, I could have filled my mind totally with Christ. I could have lived apart from others, elevating a pure spirit to God alone until the day

19. Cf. Theocritus, *Id.* 11.15.

when, in buoyant hope, I should attain my final goal. Would to God indeed. But I was overwhelmed by affection for my dear parents, and dragged earthwards by that weight. Not so much affection indeed, but pity, the tenderest of all emotions, which penetrates to the marrow of one's being. Pity for the grey hairs that were godlike, pity for their pain, their childlessness, pity too because of their child. Their tremors are for him, as they surround him, the apple of their eye,[20] the sharer of their agonies, with tender care.

Previously, books were his whole preoccupation, the books the Spirit had made by the tongues of his holy ones. Within was the shining grace of the Spirit's noble composition, the concealed treasure which is manifested only to the pure among mortals. Prayers and groans were dear to him, and sleepless nights, and the angelic choirs who stand and beseech God in psalms, elevate their souls to God in hymns while they harmonize many mouths into a single voice. Dear to him, too, the distress of that fount of evil, the belly, and moderation in laughter, control of tongue and eye, and rein on furious anger. That wanderer, the mind, which peers about everywhere, reason would keep in check. He directed it to Christ in heavenly hopes. With reason presiding over everything, leading the image to the King, God found the zealous effort pleasing.

The phantasms of the night simply reproduce one's daily preoccupations; and for me possessions and strident clamors mean bad dreams by night. Their place was taken previously by the splendor of God, which blinded my vision,[21] by the illustrious chorus and the glory of pious souls. As it is, all such treasures have vanished from a soul that once enjoyed only the company of the best.

All I have now is yearning and the hopeless pain. Hence these tears. What the morrow will bring I do not know. Will God deliver me from my woes, shake all anxieties away, and lead me again to former ways? Or will He drive me hence in

20. Gregory frequently tells us that he was the favorite child in the family.
21. Dreams have a peculiar fascination for Gregory; cf. C.M. Szymusiak-Affholder, "Psychologie et histoire dans le rêve initial de Grégoire le théologien" *Philologus* 15 (1971): 302–310.

the midst of my anxieties before I can see the dawn, before I can lay a salve to my wounds? After the depths of the night behold me thirsting for the light. Is there any succour for vain laments? In the place where mortals have their remedy, all decisions are irrevocable. Grey hairs are already upon me, and my wrinkled limbs tend towards the evening of this life of tears.

PREVIOUS WOES, 307–366

Never before have I encountered trouble of such dimensions. Not even when I was tossed by the raging winds on my way to Achaea from Alexandria. At the rising of Taurus,[22] the chief terror of sailors, a time when few venture to sea, it was my lot to voyage. For twenty days and nights I was prostrate in the prow, calling on the almighty God in prayer. From either side, like cliffs or mountains, the waves rolled upon the vessel and we shipped much water. All our tackle was shattered as the wind whistled shrilly through the sheets. The sky was black with lightning-flecked clouds,[23] and everywhere strident voices rose in clamor. It was at that moment I gave myself to God, and the sacred promises I made delivered me from the raging ocean.

Nor again, when all the foundations of spacious Greece were shaken and there seemed no shelter from disaster, and I was fearful because my soul was as yet uninitiated in heavenly rites, for lack of the salutary washing which brings to human beings the grace and illumination of the Spirit.[24] Nor when sickness filled my mouth with a foul flux, constricted my breathing and threatened my life. Nor when I unwittingly

---

22. For the storm on the way to Greece (vv.308–321) cf. the description in *Carmina de seipso*, XI.*De vita sua*, vv.130–209, n.13 *infra*.

23. On the lightning-flecked clouds cf. M. Kertsch, "Zum Motiv des Blitzes in der griechischen Literatur der Kaiserzeit," *Wiener Studien* 13 (1979): 166–174.

24. On Gregory's delay in being baptized cf. *Carmina de seipso*, XI.*De vita sua*, vv.275–281.

drove a thorn into my eyeball, and made it all bloody, while foolishly toying with a twig. My vision was destroyed, like that of a murderer, and the stupid mistake caused me great agony. I could not use my hands to offer up the sacrifice of the Spirit until my tears had healed the wound. For it is wrong to let anything unpurified touch what is holy, or to confront the burning sun with impaired vision. And I had many other mishaps as well. Who could tell my tale of trials and favors ever since my call by God? But such a sea of troubles lay in store for my hapless soul as I had never experienced before.

How that soul does yearn to see the blessed day when it is divested of all the garb of woe, when in naked purity it can flee the flame, the stranglehold of this harsh world, and the mighty maw of the dragon, whose slavering jaws lust to devour anything they grasp. My spirit is indeed the prey of Belial.[25] O for a flood from my head and from my eyes, so that rivers of tears might wash away all stains, and I bewail in due fashion my sins. The great remedy for mortals, and for darkened souls, is weeping, and ashy dust, and bare sackcloth on the ground.

Whoever sees my plight should tremble and improve his life. He should flee the dark plain of Egypt, the harsh labors and king Pharaoh,[26] and wend his way to the holy fatherland. Let him not remain captive on the rugged plains of Babylon, sitting by the riverbank and weeping as he hangs up untouched all the instruments of music.[27] But let him make haste to the confines of the holy land. Let him flee the enslaving yoke of the Assyrian, with which he was formerly oppressed,[28] and cast down with his hands the foundations of the great temple. Since to my great misfortune I abandoned that land, I have not ceased to yearn for it. But my harsh plight has plunged me into old age. I am bent to the earth, my spirits oppressed with mourning. I stand in awe of mortals and of

---

25. On Belial cf. *Carmina de seipso*, XLV.*De animae suae calamitatibus carmen lugubre*, PG 37.1354, v.16, *Or.* 24.15, *In laudem Cypriani*, PG 35.1188.
26. Cf. Ex 11–12.   27. Cf. Ps 137.1–2.
28. On the yoke of the Assyrian Cf. 2 Kgs 17.6, Gn 10.11.

the immortal King. Abject in dress, in heart, reduced to silence, in my misery I challenge the pity of the King. He is benign to all the humble, but crushes the proud.

GOOD SAMARITAN, 367–392

It is as when, according to the story, the man was going down from Jerusalem to the famous city of Jericho.[29] Wicked thieves set upon the wayfarer and used him badly. They wounded him with shameful blows, and stripping off the garments with which he was clothed, pitilessly abandoned him to die. Soon came other wayfarers, a Levite and a priest, but they too passed him by without pity. Then came a Samaritan, who had pity on him. He took him, and bandaged him, left salve for his wounds, and money for someone to nurse him. What a great portent! How was it that the Samaritan seeing him had pity, when the great ones failed to pity? I do not clearly understand what is hidden in this similitude: such mysteries does God in His wisdom conceal.[30]

May God be merciful to me. The misfortunes I encountered were like that too. Me too that robber who hates souls ill-used, as I travelled from the noble city and its way of life. He stripped me of the grace of Christ and left me naked, as once he did to Adam, the origin of flesh and fall, who by a taste was cast down to the earth whence he had sprung. O King, have pity on me. Save me from death. The priests abandoned me when they saw me in sore straits. Bind up well my wounds, and lead me to the universal inn, whence you can restore me once more intact to the holy city. There let me remain forever, while you ward off wicked thieves, the hardships of the road, wounds and wayfarers of pitiless spirit who preen themselves on their piety.

29. Cf. Lk 10.30–37.
30. Gregory's failure to understand the deeper meaning of the parable of the Good Samaritan (Lk 10.33–37) is surprising. Cf. *Carmina dogmatica*, 26, *Parabolae Christi secundum Lucam*, PG 37.497, v.5.

PUBLICAN AND PHARISEE,[31] 393-423

Two men, I am taught, went up to the temple, an overweening Pharisee who considered himself before all with God, and a publican whose heart within him was heavy because of unholy gains. The Pharisee recounted in detail his fasts, his tithings according to the law, comparing himself with the men of old, and making light of the publican in his words. The publican, however, wept, beat his breast with his hands, and, afraid to raise his eyes to the broad heaven, throne of almighty God, he turned his humble gaze to the pavement. Standing afar off, he prayed thus: "Be merciful, be merciful to thy servant who is weighted down with evil. Not the law, not tithing, nor good works will save me, nor is my assailant mistaken. I am ashamed to touch the temple with my unholy feet. Let thy grace and thy pity flow on my unworthiness, for this is the one hope. O King, thou hast provided for miserable sinners."

So they spoke. God heard both, and had pity on the one he saw afflicted, whereas the haughty one he rejected. My God, I draw courage from the fact that thus you saw and straightway judge.[32] I am that publican in your sight, all deep in sin. The help I hope for is measured by the depth of my groans. If ever my father and my dear mother did honor thee with tears, and groans, and prayers, or devote to thee even a tiny portion of their possessions, or made thee a gift of pleasing and holy sacrifices, remember them, and help. I myself have never accomplished anything worthy of thee. Drive off evil anxieties. Let me not be strangled by the thicket of thorns, or impeded, as I hasten on the heavenly road. O my strength, escort me without mishap. I am thy worshipper and thy portion.

31. Cf. Lk 18.10–14.
32. Cf. Theocritus *Id.* 2.82.

NONNA'S PROMISE, 424-466

When I was delivered from my mother's womb, she offered me to you. Ever since the day she had yearned to nurse a manchild on her knee, she imitated the cry of the holy Anna. "O King Christ, that I might have a boy for you to keep within your fold. May a son be the flourishing fruit of my birth pangs." And you, O God, granted her prayer. There followed the holy dream[33] which gave her the name. In due time you gave a son. She dedicated me as a new Samuel (if I were worthy of the name) in the temple. But now. Behold I am numbered among the profane and wanton sons of thy illustrious servant Eli,[34] who foolishly had traffic with the holy sacrifices, touched the sacred cauldrons with defiled hands, and for that reason met a harsh doom.

It was with a fairer hope she dedicated to you a portion of her offspring. With the holy books she sanctified my hands, and taking me into her arms she said these words: "This beloved child, the gift of God, soon to become a sacred victim, is a precious charge under escort to the altar. He is the offspring of Sarah,[35] late in motherhood. He is the root of the race, the product of hope and the divine promise. The priest is Abraham, and the victim, an illustrious Isaac.

Accordingly, in fulfilment of my promise, I tender thee a living victim unto God. It is for you to implement your mother's hope. Through prayer she gave you birth, and now she prays you will fulfil it all. My child, this is the noble inheritance I bestow on you in this world. And in the world to come, which is by far the best."

My mother's wish was thus. And I, while yet a child, yielded to her desires. My tender soul began to be shaped in the new mold of holiness, but the seal awaited the will of Christ who so manifestly conversed with his servant. With holy chastity

---

33. On Nonna's dream cf. *De vita sua*, n.9, *infra*.
34. On the new Samuel and Eli cf. 1 Sm 1.24, 2.12–17.
35. For Nonna as Sara cf. *Or.* 8, *In laudem sororis Gorgoniae*, PG 35.793, FOTC 22.103(4), *Epitaphia*, 27, *Anth. Pal.*, 412.

455 he bound me and put a rein upon my flesh. He breathed into me the fervent love of holy wisdom, and of monastic life, which is the first fruits of the life to be. I did not crave a rib to cherish my body, to lead me with wheedling words towards
460 the bitter taste. All my desire is directed to God, nor do I divide between Christ and a woman[36] that which is totally sprung from God. Such a manner of life, amid companions of the better sort, leads toward the strait gate by the narrow and hard path. It is a path trodden by few: it brings to God the godly, to the Unbegotten that which is begotten of earth,
465 and renders immortal that which is mortal. The very body, too, it induces to cooperate with the image of the great God, just as gleaming iron is drawn by the magnet stone.

UNFULFILLED, 467–546

Alas, what dreadful things, how punishable, my soul has undergone. Vainglorious mortals that we are, in very truth
470 how similar to the fleeting breezes is our generation. The hollow posturings of our period on this earth are like the ebb and flow of Euripus'[37] tides, where nothing maintains its character to the end. It holds for good and evil: the ways are so adjacent. For the evil man knows not what his final fate will
475 be, and virtue will not keep stable for the good. It is plagued by envy, as wickedness is by fear. It was the will of Christ that mortals should be swayed by these two forces in order that, depending on his strength, our gaze should be directed up-
480 wards. The best thing is to follow the straight path, not turning aside to the sad ashes of Sodom[38] where lust brought down the strange consuming fire. And so one flees precipitately to the mountains, forgetting fatherland, lest one's legacy for posterity become a pillar of salt and a cautionary tale.

My own career indeed gives evidence of human failing.
485 When I was a child, when the understanding in my heart was

36. Cf. 1 Kgs 2.
37. For Euripus in metaphorical sense cf. Aristotle, *Eth. Nic.* 1167b.
38. On Sodom cf. Mt 10.15, 21–22; Lk 17.29–32.

only slight, I lived in upright ways under the shadow of reason alone, and took with unfailing feet the royal road towards the seat that shines on high. But now, learned though I be and drawing towards the close of life, the course that I pursue alas, with, as it were, drunken feet, is oblique. I am weighted down by combat with the crooked demon, who openly and secretly seeks to pervert a mind that is intent on noble things. Sometimes my mind tends to God, and sometimes again it is drawn towards the evil confusion of the world. How much has not my soul been wounded by this vast world?

Nevertheless, encompassed though I be by evil blackness, even though in the past the enemy has poured out dark poison on me, as the sepia fish vomits on the waters,[39] this much perception and vision I do have, and it is the best of all.

I realize who I am, where I wish to raise myself, and where actually in my misery I lie, in what slimy earth, nay, in what broad pits beneath the earth. I am not cheered by consolations, deceived by considerations that merely minister to the passions, or self-righteous when I perceive the extent of others' wrongdoings, as if I were exemplary. Do people under torture on the rack derive any satisfaction from the harsher pains of those in a similar plight? Does the greater wickedness of others mean any profit for those who are themselves wicked?

The good man, of course, can derive benefit from the example of a better man. And so can the wicked. A person with vision is a help to those who are blind. Malicious delight in the number of the wicked denotes a deeper degree still of wickedness. But my great cross, a hidden source of lament in my heart, is when those actually wicked get the reputation of being good. Better let goodness itself have an evil reputation than let evil have a good one, for that is to be a lying sepulchre among men, to reek inwardly of putrid corpses, while gleaming on the outside with whitewash[40] and charming colors.

What we should fear is that great eye which sees beneath

---

39. On the sepia fish (σηπία) cf. Aristotle, *Hist. An.* 4.8.21; Hipponax, 62; Aristophanes, *Ach.* 351.
40. Cf. Mt 23.27.

the earth, penetrates the immense depths of the ocean and whatsoever the mind of man conceals. Nothing is obliterated by time: it is all open to God. How could anyone conceal his wrongdoing? Where shall we hide ourselves on the last day? Who will shelter us? How shall we escape the eye of God on the day when the purifying fire judges the deeds of all, and consumes the dry and crackling tinder of evil? It is evil that causes me to tremble and be afraid night and day. I see my soul fallen down towards the earth from God, and being drawn towards the matter from which I yearned to escape.

It is as when by the banks of a river in flood a pine tree or a flourishing plane[41] is torn from its roots by the passing surge and destroyed. First all the foundations are undermined, and the tree leans headlong over the bank. Then it is broken off from the slight roots by which it still clings, and it is whirled into the middle of the torrent. Amid great crackling it is borne among the rocks, where it rots under the constant wear of flood and flotsam. There it lies by the banks, a wretched trunk.

So with my soul. It was flourishing for Christ the King. But in furious onset the inexorable enemy cast it to earth. Most of it perished, and the pitiable remnant is borne hither and thither. God alone can raise it up again. He formed us out of nothing, and when hereafter we are dissolved, he will put us together again and deliver us to that other life, there to encounter either the fire or God the giver of light. Whether, finally, God be the lot of all, let us not here discuss.[42]

HOPE FOR RECOVERY, 547–595

O Christ my king, though I be called a corpse and strengthless by enemy men, though secretly they ridicule me and

---

41. For the extended metaphor (vv.530–538) of the uprooted pine or plane tree, cf. Homer, *Il.* 13.137–143, 17.53, and especially 11.492–496; see also Vergil, *Aen.* 3.659.

42. An allusion evidently to Origen's doctrine of *Apokatastasis*. Cf. J. Daniélou, *L'Être et le Temps chez Grégoire de Nysse* (Leiden 1970), 205–226.

mock my misfortune with wagging heads, do not abandon me to be subdued by violent hands. Begin by setting me up once more in heavenly hope. Replenish with a tiny drop of oil, harbinger of light for thirsty lamps, my waning flickers, so that, when the fire is again restored, the light renewed will shine once more, and I succeed in reaching to the resplendent life. Secondly, let all my woes disappear with the puffs of wind. Blow with a gentle breath, and cast from me the trials with which you have sufficiently subdued my spirit. It may be my lamentable wrongdoing that you requite. Or perhaps you are using trouble to subdue me, as one trains a colt by various exercises of endurance? Or restraining some spiritual pride on my part? Pious people of fickle mind are very liable to this, and use God's goodness as excuse for haughty and reprehensible airs. Or again, O saving Word, you may wish that men be led by my misfortunes to hate the wickedness of the world. It is no lasting word, and brings everyone, good and bad, to woe. You may wish men to make haste towards that other world, the stable, the unshaken, the proper goal of pious souls.

Such matters belong to the high levels of wisdom. Mortals learn their lesson by the good and bad, the ups and downs of living. Even though our crass minds fail to see their purpose for the most part, with the Word all things are for the best. Hither and thither, all-wisely, you bend the rudder of the universe, and with you as helmsman we traverse the rough swell of this uncertain life with all its woeful reefs.[43] And so, afflicted though I be, oppressed by all kinds of troubles, I fall to my knees before Thee. Send me Lazarus so that he may quickly refresh with his moistened finger my tongue that is parched in the flame. May I be no longer detained in the abyss. Let not Abraham shut out from his ample bosom the rich man in his agony.[44] Support me with your mighty hand,

---

43. On the imagery see B. Lorenz, "Zur Seefahrt des Lebens in den Gedichten des Gregor von Nazianz," *VigC* 33 (1979): 234–241, R. Freise, "Zur Metaphorik der Seefahrt in den Gedichten Gregors von Nazianz" in *II. Symposium Nazianzenum*, 159–163.

44. Cf. Lk 16.22–24.

provide relief from woe. Let all the wonders and the mighty portents be displayed in my regard.

Say the word, as you did formerly, and let the issue of blood be straightaway dried.[45] Say the word and let the legion of devils madden the herd of swine,[46] so that it rush into the sea and retire from me. Drive out the miserable leprosy,[47] give light to eyes that are blind and hearing to deaf ears.[48] Make the withered hand stretch out, loose the knot of the tongue, make firm the tottering gait of the feet. [49] Fill me with a morsel of bread, calm the raging sea, shine more brightly than the sun, give life to the paralyzed limbs, raise to life the rotting corpse.[50] Do not, when you look upon me, make me fruitless, as you did the barren fig tree once upon a time.[51]

FINAL PRAYER, 596-634

O Christ, people take refuge in all sorts of consolations, in blood, or ashes, or ephemeral pride. But while they cling to a support that is worthless, I alone turn to you only, O majestic one. You have power over all things and are my greatest strength. I have no loving wife to smooth away the harsh anxieties, or cheer me in affliction with kind speech. Nor can I turn to the consolation of beloved children, whose young footsteps guide and support the old in their journey. Or that of brothers and companions. My brother was snatched from me by a harsh fate. As for my companions, they were lovers of tranquillity, sensitive to a comrade's slightest hurt. That one consolation I did have, and I resorted to it as a thirsting fawn does to a cooling spring: the noblest of men, Christ-bearing, dwellers upon earth, but superior to the flesh, friends of the eternal Spirit, dignified in worship, celibate, despising the world.

45. Cf. Mk 5.29.
46. Cf. Lk 8.30.
47. Cf. Mt 8.3, Mk 1.42.
48. Cf. Mt 15.30.
49. Cf. Lk 6.6, Lk 1.64, Mt 11.5.
50. Cf. Mt 6.11, Mt 8.27, 9.6, 17.22, Jn 11.43.
51. Cf. Mk 11.12–22.

But they too, because of conflict concerning Thee, stand divided on this side and that. Their misguided zeal has transgressed the divine precept and dissolved the harmony of charity. Only the name remains. It is as if a man had just escaped a lion[52] only to find a savage bear approaching, and escaping that in turn should flee thankfully to his house. But while he leans his hand against the wall, a serpent darts from it unexpectedly and strikes him.

That is my story. Hounded by many mishaps I find no rest from weariness. What comes next is always more grievous still. So, having searched everywhere, and suffered everywhere, from Thee, O blessed one, to Thee I turn my gaze again. Thou art my strength, the Lord of all, the Unbegotten, the Beginning and the Father of the Beginning, who is the Immortal Son. Thou art the Great Light sprung from similar light, circling in a manner that is ineffable from One to One. O Son of God, Wisdom, King, Word, Truth, Image of the Archetype, Nature equal to the Begetter, Shepherd, Lamb, Victim, God, Man, Highpriest; and Spirit proceeding from the Father, Light of my mind,[53] who comest to the pure and makest God of man, look down in mercy. As the years run their course, grant that I may here and hereafter be mingled with the whole divinity. With hymns unending may I celebrate Thee in joy.

---

52. For the lion, bear and serpent cf. *Carmina de seipso*, XII.*De se ipso et de episcopis*, PG 37.1168–1169, vv. 30–35.
53. For the cumulative listing of titles for the Son cf. *Or.* 30.19, 20, 21, *De filio*, SC 250.264–274.

11 CONCERNING HIMSELF AND THE BISHOPS
De se ipso et de episcopis II/I/XII

(PG 37.1166–1227)

INTRODUCTION, 1-24

It may be that, just as I modelled myself after the commandments of him who suffered and bore with ill-use, so too, after ill-use, I should restrain my language: in the hope, that is, of the more perfect reward which recompenses a more demanding struggle. For reward is according to quality of performance, for the perfect, perfect; for the lesser, something less than perfect.[1] However I should not wish the wicked to be altogether triumphant, or their path made smooth without a protesting voice being raised.

I am content to leave their ultimate fate to the final conflagration[2] because it will test and purge all things impartially, however much people manage to escape in this world by subterfuges. For my part I propose to give a minor tongue-lashing to my assassins, for that is what they are, those framers of monstrous judgments, who shed the blood of innocent souls I myself molded and developed. I shall say what I have to say without fear of recrimination, though that is something everyone wishes to avoid and that I find particularly hateful. In the course of my remarks I do not propose to mention names, lest I seem to be indulging in criticism in domains that ought to be confidential. And, for fear my tongue should run away with me, I shall not recount all details at equal length.

BAD AND GOOD BISHOPS, 25-70

I realize that there are many persons who deserve high commendation. At the present juncture the one who must be

---

1. An allusion to Purgatory apparently. See J. Mossay, *La mort et l'au-delà dans saint Grégoire de Nazianze*, Univ. de Louvain Rec. de trav. d'hist. & de philol. 4ᵉ Ser. XXXIV (Louvain Bib. de l'Univ. 1966).
2. Cf. 1 Cor 3.13.

apprehended and subdued is the one who is in the camp of the wicked, or worse than wicked. The sword of the tongue shall smite the miscreant, and who the miscreant is you will make manifest. You shall stand as your own accuser if you find yourself at variance with this account. Since this is my attitude, let whoever wishes open fire, because long ago I have become inured to stonings. Now of the lion one need have no fear, the leopard is a gentle creature, and even the snake you are terrified by is likely to turn in flight;[3] but there is one thing you must beware of, I assure you. Bad bishops. Don't be overawed by the dignity of the throne. All have the dignity, yes; but not all have the grace. Discard the outer clothing; watch for the wolf.[4] Words do not convince me; I must have deeds.

Teachings that are rendered null by lives I abominate. I must praise the outer coloring of the sepulchre;[5] but the stench of rotten bodies within disgusts me. But how, and why, you say? How can a man like you, who invariably deals in fair speech, fail to do so also now? Indeed it is with pain that I set down this wretched story for God, for friends, for parents, for neighbors, for strangers, and if for them, also for the generations yet to come.

I shall go back some distance in the story. No one should ever say that laborers have any profit from their toil: that is a delusion. It is all a weary pilgrimage through darkness and mist. God tries some by fire,[6] and over some he casts a darkness until the day when fire casts light on all things. You have, on the one hand, a man who has eked out a life of toil. Groans, vigils, limbs wasted by tears, the constraints of fasting and of a hard pallet by night, anxieties of the spirit, study of sacred writ, constant laceration by interior scourges—did I escape any of these things? Was I guilty of a single untoward act? On the other hand, you have the man who plucked the joys of youth. He sported, he sang, he pandered to the ap-

---

3. Lions, bears and snakes recur as greater menaces in *Carmina de seipso*, I.*De rebus suis*, PG 37.1015–1017, vv.616–619.
4. Cf. Aesop, *The Wolf in Sheep's Clothing* in *Babrius and Phaedrus*, Loeb, ed. B. E. Perry (Cambridge, Ma., 1965) 513.451; Mt 7.15.
5. Cf. Mt 23.27.
6. Again, Purgatorial fire. But cf. 1 Cor 3.15.

petites of the belly, he surrendered to all pleasures, unlocked the door to all sensations, was a colt without restraint. And in the end it is the former who is dogged by disaster. Nay, not disaster. Common estimation has it that the wise man is impervious to the calamities of life; but common estimation makes away with even the semblance of wisdom. Our friend who had the smooth course all the way is successful in the domain of reputation too. He's considered virtuous. The author of the tale which follows can bear witness that the pattern is so.

CALL TO CONSTANTINOPLE, 71–114

There was a time when I was set on high, above all things of perception, my mind concerned with the intelligibles only. Renown had been laid aside, as well as possessions, prospects and eloquence. My luxury was to eschew luxury: I sweetened my life with frugal leaven. I was safe from contumely; because however wise one may be one must expect anything.

But, unexpectedly, an upright person[7] whose name I cannot mention snatched me away and exiled me. Was it the Holy Spirit, or just my sins, that I might pay the penalty of eminence? There was an ostensible occasion indeed, a synod of bishops, and a congregation that was orthodox but limited as yet. Recently the congregation had been raising their gaze a little to the rays of the sun, so that some measure of confidence should be restored to true doctrine, and a respite gained from the encircling evils of babbling tongues and complicated errors,[8] before the onset of which they were defenseless. This was the manner of my coming, a godly stranger, to bloom like a fragrant rose in the midst of brambles, or a single ripe grape in an unripe cluster. It was their protestations and prayers of every kind that swayed me; to have resisted them would be unduly proud.

7. *i.e.*, Basil.
8. Arians and Apollinarists. Cf. P. R. Rudasso, *La figura di Christo in S. Gregorio Nazianzeno* (Rome 1968), 53–65.

I left the land of Cappadocia, that bastion of orthodoxy in the eyes of everyone, and arrived unequipped with any of the things I needed (lying stories to the contrary are the concoctions of enemies to furnish a crude cloak for their spite).

The rest of the story I should like you people to tell, you who can bear witness to my labors. For three years now have I said or done anything harsh, untoward, or injurious? It is true, of course, that I did show one weakness: I spared those miscreants at whose hands I endured stoning at the very outset. When subjected to the same sufferings as Christ, it seemed the more Christian thing to emulate his patience. You see, then, the sort of offering to God that is within the gift of the poor. Another matter, too, might indeed be construed as a fault. Someone has remarked that an anxious mind is a moth which gnaws the bones;[9] that is something I've come to realize by experience. This frame of mine, once stalwart, has withered under anxiety and grown bent already. My strength is exhausted, and even when I put forth every effort I am less than adequate. What a fate it is to be yoked to a friend-body that is unsound.

HIS EARLY MINISTRY, 115–135

But I must return to the story I had begun. I received my call. In the midst of wolves I built up a congregation. I watered this parched flock with doctrine, and I sowed the seeds of a faith that is rooted in God. I lit the lamp of the Trinity for people hitherto in darkness; a persuasive tongue made me a potent flavor in the milk. Some I had already firmly attached to myself; others were on the point of attachment, and others still were due to come. The temper of the general body, which had been turbulent formerly, had become mild; and teaching was sweetened with charity. A little impetus, and there were prospects of complete success.

9. Cf. Philo, *De posteritate Caini*, 56, *De somniis*, 1.77, Aristophanes, *Lys.*, 729.

The flourishing city of Rome is well aware of this, especially, I maintain, the prominent people there, [10] who held me in no small esteem. And so much superior to all others are such folk that to have even slight repute with them means more than primacy of honor elsewhere. May they live long! They held me in respect while I was there, and now that I am gone they blame my opponents. It is all that they can do indeed, nor should I require them to do more. Alas, poor city, if I may indulge in tragic exclamation.[11]

RESIGNATION, 136–175

Envy, however, rent apart those gentlemen, my fellow bishops. You know the character of Thracians,[12] a provincialism that is impervious to training. To bolster their case they used my bodily infirmity, which had been brought on by overwork. People who had labored even a little for the Lord ought, of course, to have respected this circumstance. They should have reflected that, with the world split in acrimonious dispute, the eminence of such a throne held no attraction. Under the impulse of the demon though, they avidly seized upon the pretext and sent me forth. Like ballast from an overloaded ship I was jettisoned, because my moderate sentiments proved a nuisance for the enemy. And, after all that, they presume to raise their hands in righteousness to God, to send up purifying oblations from the heart, to sanctify with mystic words the faithful, those very people who wickedly got rid of me. But I was a willing victim indeed: the shame of being associated with such hucksters[13] of the faith would be intolerable.

---

10. *i.e.*, Theodosius. Cf. *Carmina de seipso*, XI.*De vita sua*, PG 37.1029, vv.15–16.
11. Cf. Sophocles, *OT*, 629, B. Wyss, *RAC* 12.846. The poem has many echoes of this play.
12. There seems to be a play on *Thrason*, the stock name in New Comedy for the braggart soldier, as in Menander, *Misumenos*, "Thrasonides"; cf. B. Wyss, *RAC*.12.849.
13. Gregory indulges in a certain amount of snobbery here (vv.155–175) about the inferior social backgrounds of some of the bishops. B. Wyss (*RAC* 12.849) sees here the influences of Old Comedy as well as Cynic diatribe. See

155 Some of them are the offspring of tribute-mongers, whose only concern is falsification of accounts. Some come straight from the tax booth and the sort of statutes you get there: some from the plough, with their sunburn still fresh: some again from day-long exertions with the mattock and the hoe: 160 some have just left the galleys or the army. They are still redolent of the bilge water, or exhibit the brand on their bodies;[14] but they have blossomed into captains of the people, and generals resolved not to yield an inch. Then there are those who, as yet, have not washed the soot of their fiery occupa- 165 tions from their persons, slave material who ought to be in the mills. In the old days, before they could scrape together a ransom for their masters they would get little enough respite from hard labor. But now you can't hold them back, and either by persuasion or intimidation they've succeeded in 170 filching away a section of the people. So these heaven-bound dung beetles continue their ascent; but their vehicle is no longer from the dung-heap, nor are they upside down like in the old days. They think they have the power of heaven- 175 ly beings themselves, and keep spouting pernicious stuff, though they're unable to count their hands or their feet.

WHAT IS A BISHOP,[15] 176–191

I ask you, is not all this outrageous, and unworthy of the office of a bishop? However much we are concerned about humility, let's not be so silly as to take a lowly view of that 180 office, which is no mean thing. A bishop should be from among the best, indeed, let me say it openly, he should be the very best! It follows that he should certainly not be the very

---

T. A. Kopeček, "The Social Class of the Cappadocian Fathers," *ChH* 42 (1973): 453–466.

14. Cf. Lucian, *Syr. D.*, 59, A. M. Harmon, ed., *Lucian*, Loeb, 8 vols. (Cambridge, Ma. 1961) 4: 408 and 409, n.2.

15. For Gregory's ideas on the requisite qualities of a bishop (vv.181–215) see J. Plagnieux, *Grégoire théologien*, 73–80, J. Rousse, *DSp* VI. 954, J. Bernardi, SC 247.38–50.

worst. Especially so, if my opinion is of any value, at this time of unbridled tongues where the most formidable cities and assemblies[16] are in debate. If they hold steadfast, the gain is great; and if they do not, the loss is proportionately serious. Accordingly good people must be chosen. A person of average equipment will have to struggle very hard to overcome people of that ilk: honest assessment can lead to no other conclusion.

APOSTLES AS BISHOPS, 192-261

But I shall be confronted, of course, by the fishermen and publicans who were evangelists.[17] Though barren of eloquence their simple preaching drew the universe into the net, and even the wise were caught, which makes the miracle of preaching greater still. Such a line of argument is very ready on the lips of many. My reply is brief indeed, but unmistakeable.

Let me have someone with the qualities of faith of an apostle. He is without money, without wallet, without staff, half-naked, unshod as well, living for the day, rich only in hope.[18] He is not the sort of man to court the reputation of persuasive speaker, lest he seem to depend on that for his effect. He has no time for secular learning.[19] Give me such a man and I shall swallow all deficiencies; he may be inarticulate, base, lowly, a herdsman. His character veils every failing. And if you be a man like that I shall raise you to the choirs of angels, even though you be a fisherman of frogs.[20] Just tell

16. *i.e.*, Constantinople and Antioch.
17. Cf. Mt 4.18, 21; Mt 10.3.   18. Cf. Mt 10.10.
19. On Gregory's attitude to secular learning, affected by Julian's edict excluding Christians from teaching in the schools, cf. B. Wyss, *RAC* 12.816, J. Coman, "Hellénisme et christianisme dans le 25ᵉ Discours de Saint Grégoire de Nazianze," *StPatr* XIV, 3 (=TU 117) (Berlin 1976): 290–301, R. Dostalova, "Christentum und Hellenismus. Zur Herausbildung einer neuen kulturellen Identität im 4. Jahrhundert," *BySl* 44 (1982): 1–12.
20. On the fishing-frog see Aristotle *Gen. An.* 749a, Aelian, *NA* 9.24, 13.5.

me one thing: can you exorcise devils, deliver a man from leprosy, or the dead from the tomb; does the paralytic have his limbs restored by you, or does the touch of your hand on the ailing drive out disease?[21] It is by those means you will persuade me to hold learning in small esteem.

But when two elements go to make up something, one commendable, the other to be deprecated, and you take account of one only, deliberately passing over the other, you are straining the similitude very reprehensibly. True, Matthew was a publican;[22] but he was respected not in his capacity as publican, but because he was suffused by the Spirit. Peter was the head of the disciples;[23] but he was Peter, not in his capacity as netsman, but because he was full of zeal. Even the net I can respect because of his character. From you, however, I turn away, even though you have dignified trappings, which amount to a snare and hunter's trap. You're like a painter who's capable only of reproducing the blemishes and defects of a beautiful model. Reproduce all the beauty, or leave the model alone.

Furthermore, answer me this. Can you describe as untutored the authors of writings the tiniest obscurity of which I, who have long been trained in letters, must labor to elucidate. On those writings so much study and labor have been expended that the whole world is filled with commentaries in every language,[24] works of superior quality, fruitful, the highest flights of exegesis. If the authors had not a measure of the cultivation you are unprepared to allow them, how did they succeed in persuading kings and cities and assemblies, people who accused them, questioned them in their words, before tribunals, in crowded theaters? Their audiences were composed of wise men, lawyers, haughty Greeks; but their timely speech was persuasive; they confuted with full confidence. If

---

21. Cf. Mk 3.15, Mt 10.8.   22. Cf. Mt 10.3.
23. Cf. Mt 10.2.
24. On Scriptural commentaries in Gregory's time and the extent of his readings cf. *Philocalia 1–20*, M. Harl, ed., SC 302 (1983) and *Philocalia 21–27*, E. Junod, ed., SC 226 (1976).

only they had not been sharers of a doctrine which you would deny.

The power of the Spirit, you might retort, and you would be right. But consider the implications. Are not you a sharer in the Spirit as well, surely that is your proudest boast? When people come seeking doctrine then, why do you begrudge them? You are prepared to allow inspiration to the Spirit, and to these men the quality of being inspired which made them appear wise. But such concession is futile really. You simply get hopelessly involved in your own arguments, by making facile assertions about things that were better kept private and unspoken. Silent, indeed I know, is the spirit of the adversary, and better silence than evil speech. O Word of God, that thou wouldst loose the tongues of those who speak justice, and bear down upon those who give vent to the hissings of serpents and to fratricidal venom.

WELL-FORMED, CANDID SPEAKERS, 262–329

So much for your argument, which is the sort one expects from the ignorant. Let me give a brief exposition of what one must take as the real facts here. Those men *were* well-trained, outstandingly so, but not in the sense of making a display. It works this way. All composition is twofold really, made up of thought and expression. Expression is like an outer garment: thought is the body which it clothes.

In some compositions both elements are good, in others one element or the other; or it may happen that the whole thing is bad, like its author's training. When we compose, the outer element gets little consideration but the inner one a great deal; because for us salvation depends upon that inner element, the thought.

But it must of course be expressed and communicated. A stopped-up spring is not of much use, or sunlight obscured by clouds: so with wisdom that is inarticulate. When a rose is sheathed by its calyx the beauty does not appear; but when the winds dissolve the calyx and the bud is displayed, then we perceive its charm.[25] If the beauty were always sheathed what would become of the celebrated charms of spring?

The expression we require is simply that of straightforward speakers. If your style is otherwise, let me discern in you the inspiration of the apostles—I should like a tincture of your enlightenment. If the doctrine set down in writing amounts to nothing, then how did I waste so much time counting in vain the sands of the sea,[26] joining night to day in my endeavor to bring some learning to these wrinkles. If those writings are worthwhile, as indeed they are, then do not abandon to the spiders the works the good have wrought.

Your style may be pedestrian, your speech rustic, it makes no difference to me. I, too, know the lowly pathways. A frugal table often pleases me more than one decked out artificially with dainties. The same with clothes, natural beauty is so much superior to what artifice can produce. Give full rein to the thought, and I am satisfied: let those who like that sort of thing have ornament, it counts for nothing.

Don't entangle me in the language of a Sextus or a Pyrrho:[27] deuce take Chrysippus, and let the Stagirite stay far away:[28] don't attempt to imitate the smooth style of Plato. If you disapprove of a person's ideas, reject his ornamental style as well. Do your philosophizing in simple language, and, however untutored your style, you will satisfy me.

Provided you instruct me, then you may teach in any style you wish. Tell me what the Trinity is, how God is one but yet divided, one majesty, one nature, a unity and a trinity. What

---

25. For the Rose and Calyx image cf. *Carmina de seipso*, XLV. *De animae suae calamitatibus carmen lugubre*, PG 37. 1371, v.250; see also F. W. Norris, "Of Thorns and Roses," 455–464.

26. For the image of measuring the sea in a cyathus cf. *Or.* 28.27, *De theologia*, SC 250.160.

27. On Sextus and Pyrrho see also *Or.* 21.12, *In laudem Athanasii*, SC 270.134 and n.1.

28. He is thinking especially of the Arian usage of Aristotelian and Stoic logic; cf. *Or.* 27.1, *Adversus Eunomianos*, SC 250.72 and n.1, B. Wyss, *RAC* 12.820, *Or.* 25.6, *In laudem Heronis philosophi*, SC 284.170 and n.1, *Carmina Moralia* 10, *De virtute*, PG 37.684, vv.47–49, *Or.* 7.20, *Funebris in laudem Caesarii fratris oratio*, PG 35.781. For Aristotle see B. Wyss, *RAC* 12.827–829.

CONCERNING HIMSELF AND THE BISHOPS 59

is the nature of angels, of the twofold world, how providence is righteous even though much seems unjust to the multitude? What is the principle of soul, of body, of the old and new testaments? What is this incarnation that so far transcends understanding, this mingling of disparate elements towards a single glory, the dying towards resurrection, the return to heaven?[29] How explain the resurrection itself, the judgment: what will be the life of the just, of sinners? Tell me, if in the Spirit you have any glimmering of an explanation, what is the principle of change in the universe, of stability? A full explanation, a partial one, or a deficient one, according to the limits of your mental purification; don't deny me this. But if you are completely blind, why in your sightless state presume to guide? What a darkness besets people whose teacher is himself blind. How both are doomed to fall together into the pit of ignorance.

BISHOPS NOW, 330–370

Well, that is one group. They constitute indeed a lesser evil; because ignorance, though bad, is a lesser evil. What is one to say though, when one thinks of the really evil people? Because there are such: there are certain wretched folk, miserable and abominable monsters, ambiguous with regard to their faith, whose norm is opportunity, not the law of God. In them as channels doctrine will flow either way: they are twisted growths, flatterers of women, disseminators of seductive venom, lions among little folk, craven before the powerful. At every table they make mighty fine parasites;[30] and the thresholds worn by them are not those of the wise but those of the powerful. What wins favor is their concern, not what

---

29. Gregory deals with many of these topics in his *Carmina dogmatica*, 1 (*De patre*), PG 37.397–401, 2 (*De filio*), PG 37.401–408, 3 (*De spiritu sancto*), PG 37.408–415, 4 (*De mundo*), PG 37.415–425 5 (*De providentia*), PG 37.424–429, 8 (*De anima*), PG 37.446–456, 9 (*De testamentis et adventu Christi*), PG 37.456–464, 10 (*De incarnatione adversus Apollinarium*), PG 37.464–470.

30. There is a similar characterization in *Or.* 27.2, *Adversus Eunomianos*, SC 250.72–74.

does good, because they want to make their neighbor evil like themselves.

345 Would you like a specimen of their brand of wisdom? This one boasts about his noble birth, that one about his eloquence, another about his wealth, still another about his family. Those distinguished for nothing else get noted for their villainy. Ig-
350 norant themselves, to have succeeded in muzzling the articulate was a clever dodge. So clever of you, gentlemen. I daresay if you felt your hands or your eyes challenged, you'd see to it that we were deprived of those faculties too.

Is not this sort of thing a manifest outrage, downright in-
355 jurious; and is it to be tolerated? What a mystery really: the splendid wave of salvation from God which pervades practically the whole universe in our day, as against the very wretched bishops who constitute our lot. I am going to make a statement that is far from pleasant, but only too true. The ordinary stage, alas, is better conducted than we are; and though I blush at having to describe the state of affairs I shall
360 do so. The empty masks of yesterday are the actors of today, and we who are set up as masters of virtue constitute a den of thieves. Should we seem to hold our tongues, our very si-
365 lence would be eloquent: "Villainy is at the helm; let no one exert himself, just be a villain, it's the best and shortest way." The norm is what people are wont to do. Even with the shaping of good mentors it's difficult enough for people to get
370 directed towards higher things. But should a man have a villainous model, as inevitably as water must flow downwards, he is caught.

HASTY CHOICE, 371–394

And the cause? The eagle they say, when he sees his young in the light of the sun, can make an admirable judgment, distinguishing the legitimate from the other.[31] The latter he casts

31. Cf. Pliny, *HN* 10.3.10, H. Rackham, ed., *Pliny*, Loeb, 10 vols. (Cambridge, Ma. 1956) 3:298, who tells us that only the "sea-eagle (*haliaëtus*) com-

out, but becomes a father to the former. Now we, on the other hand, indiscriminately elevate to bishoprics anyone and everyone, provided only they are willing. We pay no attention to previous performance, recent or long-standing, to behavior, to learning, to associations, not even the attention one needs to distinguish the rattle of a false coin.

People whose worth has not been demonstrated by the test of time, or fire, appear spontaneously as candidates for thrones. If he only realized that, for the most part, people elevated are worsened by power, who in his right senses would put forward a person he does not know? Considering that the control of oneself throughout the crises of life is such a great task, can you possibly entrust the fate of so many people to the chance comer, unless the idea be deliberately to wreck the whole craft? How is it that precious stones are hard to find, fertile land rare, bad horses everywhere, and good ones bred only in rich stables; but that you can find a bishop anywhere, totally untrained, but all ready-made in dignity?

EXAMPLES, 395–453

What a sudden change of role is made. The business of the Lord depends upon a roll of dice: or a comic mask is suddenly thrust upon some utterly trivial and insignificant creature, and behold we have an infant prodigy, a saint. With a beloved Saul like that among the prophets,[32] the grace of the Spirit must indeed be considerable. You, sir, were a mime in the public theater yesterday (I leave to others the investigation of your career outside the theater): today you provide us with an extraordinary spectacle all by yourself. And you, sir, a

---

pels its still unfledged chicks by beating them to gaze full at the rays of the sun, and, if it notices one blinking and with its eyes watering, flings it out of the nest as a bastard and not true to stock, whereas one whose gaze stands firm against the light it rears." For the same story see also Aristotle, *Hist. An.* 9.34.620, Aelian, *NA* 2.26, D'Arcy W. Thompson, *A Glossary of Greek Birds* (Oxford 1895), 26, *s.v.* "ἁλιαίετος".

32. Cf. 1 Sm 10.11.

horse-lover the other day,³³ sending clouds of dust to high heaven, instead of the prayers and pious sentiments others send. And this is the reason: some jockey fell, I dare say, or some horse got only a second, and when you got a whiff of equine air you took leave of your senses. But you're a solid citizen these days, nothing but decorum in your mien—if you don't take a secret canter back along the old trail, that is. A branch that is being trained will revert to its original state, I rather think, once the restraint is removed.

And you, sir, were a pleader up to recently. You did good business in the courts, twisting the law this way and that. You were proficient at ruining people whom justice might have delivered, because your standard for justice was the fattest fee. And now you're a judge, a Daniel all of a sudden.³⁴ You, who used to dispense justice under the sign of the naked sword, making legitimist brigandry of the bench, tyrannizing most of all over the very law itself, have become all gentle now. Apparently you change your character as readily as other people their clothes. The other day you went about with effeminate dancers, you performed at weddings with a chorus of Lydian girls, crooning ditties and getting high in your cups. And now you're the counsellor of virgins and matrons; but your former behavior makes your virtue somewhat questionable I fear. Today's Simon Peter is the Simon Magus³⁵ of yesterday: it's all too precipitate, this transformation from fox to lion.

And you, my good man, a tax official or ex-military man of some kind, do tell me how a poor man like you came to surpass in income Cyrus the Mede, or Croesus, or Midas?³⁶ Your house is enriched by the miseries of others. You changed over

---

33. In *Or.* 43.3, *Funebris oratio in laudem Basilii Magni Caesareae in Cappadocia episcopi*, PG 36.492, FOTC 22.29(3), NPNF ser. 2, 7.396, he tells us that Cappadocia is equally famous for fine horses and fine youths.

34. Cf. Dn 13.   35. Cf. Acts 8.9.

36. For Croesus, Cyrus, and Midas see *s.vv. OCD* [299], [308], [686]. Croesus was the last king of Lydia, whose wealth was legendary. He was defeated by Cyrus (Herodotus I.71) who greatly extended the Achaemenid Persian Empire. Midas was a legendary Phrygian king who received from Dionysus the gift of turning everything he touched to gold.

to the sanctuary, got hold of the throne, and proceeded to plunder indiscriminately. You wind up by lording it over the very mysteries of God, which one should only have the courage even to contemplate after lengthy preparatory training.

But you were transformed perhaps by the purification of Baptism?[37] Wait and see. Why should I begrudge you, the gain is all mine? Let time have its say. I'm only asking you to stipulate a reasonable period. You are cleansed today, yes, by the gift of God. But should you be careless enough to plunge into the same abyss, should the fount of previous wrongdoing continue to exist, be very sure that tears can be shed over your salvation. (Baptism is not by any means a transformation of character, nor does it purge the growths that spring from character.) Furthermore, prior to Baptism one still has high expectations; but subsequent to it not even these. One God, one grace.

WHAT IS NECESSARY, 454–540

Not to be evil; is that sufficient in itself? We are pleased at the obliteration of a previous impression on wax, provided a good one be substituted. You must be like Zachaeus.[38] Be good enough to make restoration to those you have wronged. The exact amount, not a penny more; because you are really unequal to doing what the law enjoins. Give whatever sum you wish to the poor.[39] Then you will be entertaining Christ in a worthy fashion. But to store up spoils and give but stingily to the poor, thinking yourself generous the while, amounts to simony,[40] if I may say so without blasphemy. Would it be fair

---

37. For Gregory's teaching on baptism, cf. *Or.* 39, *In sancta lumina*, PG 36.336–360, *Or.* 40, *In sanctum baptisma*, PG 36.360–425, NPNF ser.2, 7.352–377, D.F. Winslow, "Orthodox Baptism—A Problem for Gregory of Nazianzus," *St Patr* XIV,3 (=TU 117) (Berlin 1976): 371–374.
38. On Zachaeus cf. Lk 19.2, 8–10.
39. For Gregory's option for the poor cf. his *Or.* 14, *De pauperum amore*, PG 35.857–909, D.F. Winslow, "Gregory Nazianzenus and his love for the poor," *Anglican Theological Review* 47 (1965): 348–350.
40. Cf. Acts 5.1–12.

if my wounds should remain unhealed, while grace in your case has the effect of releasing you from obligations contracted through your wrongdoing? You have grace? Then keep away from what is not yours, and your purification will be complete. You may be full of grace; but if, instead of divesting yourself completely, you continue to hold on to what is not yours, I shudder for the outcome. And I think it's quite clear to everyone.

You desire the state of grace. But, however high you happen to be raised by the throne, I know you to be a debtor in fact. It is our past sins, not our present ones, that are wiped out by Baptism. It would be well for you to get completely purified, instead of this grotesque performance: presuming, while sullied yourself, to purify others. You're surely not going to claim you have a special privilege from God, like a special indulgence from a monarch, of commendation for the tyranny you exercise. If then, as I said, not even Baptism itself will absolutely purify those in the bond of its grace (for God is never outwitted by anyone and will deal with the clever by being cleverer still); who will cleanse from post-baptismal sins? People become sullied again in the abyss of filth. They desecrate the dignity of the image from above with the forms of beasts and creeping things; for by imitation we are formed into the likeness of these. And our character too continues to mold us: it is a difficult task to uproot this and cast it away. There is no second purifying.[41]

One (baptismal) birth was vouchsafed me, and at that time I was molded unto God. Perhaps, hereafter, when cleansed by the beneficial fire, I may be molded in another shaping; but in this world I know no remedy except tears. They do produce, but with difficulty, some healing for the wounds. In my view though, the scars continue to remain, as evidence of what once were gaping wounds. If someone has more confidence in the mercy of God than I do, all the better for me;

---

41. See C. Moreschini, "Luce e purificazione nella dottrina di Gregorio Nazianzeno," *Augustinianum* 13 (1973): 535–549.

but he must prove his point. It might be argued perhaps that there is a sort of purifying grace in the episcopal ministrations themselves, in public proclamation, the sort of things that, all unworthy, we promulgate.[42] That is to attribute cleansing power to the ceremony and to the overpowering influence doubtless of the Spirit. It is the view of good and wise bishops.

I am inclined to think, however, that the likelihood of contracting defilement is greater than that of gaining further brilliance. It's easier to get involved in evil than in good. How true this is you can realize from the statement of Michaeas:[43] that, should consecrated meat touch any other food or drink, it will never sanctify what it touches, whereas the touch of the unholy will render what is holy common. Saint Paul, too, in the epistle to Timothy is firmly convinced of this.[44] He lays down the principle that hands are not to be imposed on another lightly, nor is one to communicate in his evil ways; because our own failings are burden enough for us.

If you wish though, let's grant you this baptismal purification. Who is going to guarantee your character until sufficient time has elapsed to indicate that grace has gone down to the depths, that the shining front is not only skin-deep, like one of those herbal dyes where the beauty can be washed away? Granted even that the purification be absolute. Your elevation has transformed you, yes, and I'm confronted by an angel. This, one of the faithful, who observes the laws which I do and accepts the teaching, will readily concede. A non-believer, however, has only one yardstick for measuring the quality of religious faith, good reputation. He may not take the slightest reckoning of his own shortcomings, but he is a stringent critic of yours. And, tell me, how can we set up in his eyes a reputation other than the one we had before? By what arguments can we stop his mouth? On my principles, this is an aspect we

---

42. Episcopal consecration probably consisted of a public proclamation with the laying on of hands. It is argued that this conveys the necessary charism.
43. A slip by Gregory. The reference is actually to *Haggai*, 2.13–14.
44. Cf. 1 Tm 5.22.

cannot overlook: I would have the image of the bishop a polished one from every angle, lest the faithful suffer.

IS GRACE SUFFICIENT? 541–574

But grace is stronger than reputation: this even I shall allow to pass. All stand in awe of you: not a shadow of blame falls on you: on those presumptuous premises of yours you're second only to Elias. You take your lofty seat, completely ignorant and unaware of considerations that cause many people concern and anxiety. I should be astonished indeed if they were of concern to you: your vanity, by which you are so easily persuaded to baseless pretensions, doesn't allow you to become aware of them.

But you're clear on this score. Very well: can you avoid though, being master and pupil at one and the same time, whetting the whetstone, like hogs with their tusks? Your obligation is first thoroughly to learn the law, and then to teach. A nice mess it all now is, however, did doctrine get reduced to this cheap level? There aren't any boxers who haven't had previous training and made a study in good time of contests. Do you find a track-runner who hasn't exercised his legs? Did anyone in his senses ever cut pipes, shape them, and enter a contest all on the same day? Did you ever hear of a first-rate painter who did not initially experiment with several colors? Of a rhetor without experience of speeches, a doctor without experience of diseases? If the mere wish were sufficient for their possession, skills like these would be of very little value indeed.

A bishop, however, only needs the call, and he is an expert straightway. It's a signal instance of the saying being the doing. Christ commands and something springs into being! There's a consideration, too, that I don't want to labor. How can you presume to raise your head and aspire to the power of the throne, when you are conscious of a servant of God continuing to sit below you. You ought to tremble and cower where you sit, because you may be leading a flock who are better than their shepherd.

THE GOOD SHEPHERD, 575–609

Give yourself time to consider what I am here depicting: You have this man who sleeps on the ground and is all befouled with dust. He has worn his body away with keeping vigils, with psalmody, with standing night and day.[45] He has drawn his mind away from all crassness towards the heights; there being no point, he thinks, in bringing the whole carcass to the tomb, just to provide more elaborate nourishment for the worms it shall produce, and nourish when produced. He has washed away all the stains with rivers of tears, and any tiny speck he retained of that mud of life which spatters even the wise. He bears the noble seal of flesh that has been worn by prayer and countless hardships, the hardship which men returned again to lowly mother earth must endure since the ancient tasting.

In cold, in hunger, and in wretched garments, he yearns to put on the clothing that is imperishable. With insufficient food he does violence to the belly's pride, each day summoning death to mind, because he has knowledge of God, the simple nourishment of the angels. Once he was a rich man, but now he is poor; for he is making life's voyage without cargo. That he decided to jettison, not to the depths, but to the poor. From cities, from the plaudits of the mob, from the whirl in which all public life is tossed, he is a fugitive. His fair soul he has molded towards God, and in his absolute solitude partakes of heavenly things only. His body's beauty (and could the body of the best be other than beautiful) he has enclosed, oysterwise, in the secret adornment of iron chains. He, though completely guiltless, has put himself in bonds, for fear his freedom should ever give offense; and his wandering senses he has put in thrall within himself. To him the Spirit

---

45. Cf. *Panegyric on Athanasius, Or.* 21.10, *In laudem Athanasii*, PG 35.1093.

has disclosed the deeper meaning of Holy Writ, uncovering all that is sealed to the understanding of the multitude.

THE UNWORTHY SHEPHERD, 610-651

610 Can you claim that such a picture describes you? No, what you have is a complete establishment, an attractive wife to be the mother of your children, property, stewards, collectors of tribute, clamor, lawsuits, anxiety and activity everywhere. Your table groans under the most recherché artifices and menus of cooks, who titivate your appetite with the fruits of land and sea, that combine to submerge and circumscribe the spirit. Perfumes and gaity surround you, and the sort of psalms that go with cymbals and foot tapping.

620 Or there are those who are slaves to the natural lusts. Indulgence with women makes them sleek and swollen; husbands who have anticipated the bridal bower is the kindest description of them. They may be already in dalliance with premarital loves, though their cheeks are still unadorned with the manly ornament of hair. In their first down indeed, they are immature in body, but in character still more immature. Or, at the other extreme, they are ancient of days and full of vices. And they set themselves up as leaders for children who are not of the flesh, children whom the Spirit, that is stranger to the flesh, brings forth. The passions they have themselves experienced they have learned to appreciate; and in dealing with the sins of others they become advocates for themselves, at once allowing, and being allowed, license.

635 Such is the pattern. People like that might perhaps improve their conduct, but their thrones stand in the way. Folly is simply intensified by power. Meanwhile there stands your man of self-control in obscurity. He is modestly bowed, his gaze directed exclusively to God; and he chooses the role of disciple though his master of the moment (unless we make position the touchstone of authority) is not perhaps worthy to be even his disciple. To such extent has the evil one come to

hold sway among us: by such clever wiles he makes his inroads whenever he has the whim to ensnare a people or a city.[46] As well as tempting each individual, he popularizes vice by means of some fashionable custom. Gold is simply a veneer for bronze: color, chameleon-fashion, is changed. We have the beard, the humble mien, the bowed head, the subdued voice, the contrived sincerity, the measured gait; everything that goes with wisdom indeed, except a wise mind.

BISHOPS' FASHIONS, 652–708

Among fashionable affectations of our time the venerable ephod[47] comes first. Then there's the linen apron of Samuel,[48] an inconspicuous litter not fully caparisoned, headdress in virginal linen, with sackcloth to give the outward semblance of prayer. It's difficult to avoid resorting to language foreign to my style. I cannot help it, any more than I can contain my indignation. Your life of luxury or your hairstyle: one or the other, sir, you should curtail. Don't try to affect simultaneously what is native to you and what is not; the lands of the Mysians and the Phrygians are much divided, the waters of Merra and of Siloe far apart. The former are undrinkable;[49] but when an angel moves the latter, even diseases are cured. Yours is a double sowing, an ambiguous vine. You've made your coat of two materials and are trying to stitch together what won't go together. What was compounded was forbidden under the law you realize: it was averse to duplicity. Between proper adornment for women and for men there is a distinction,[50] or between the highest reach of crows and that of eagles. Aping the great is disgraceful when one is an insig-

---

46. Cf. Sophocles, frag. 273, ed., Mette, 16, B. Wyss, *RAC* 12.846.
47. For the ephod cf. *DicBib* 2.1865. The ephod, the vest, worn by the Old Testament high priest, had twelve gems representing the twelve tribes. See also Ex 28.6–14.
48. For the linen apron (διπλοΐς) of Samuel cf. 1 Sm 2.18.
49. Cf. Ex 15.23.
50. Cf. Clement of Alexandria, *Paidagogos* 2.10.106, GSC 1.221.3 and 332.25, B. Wyss, *RAC* 12.848.

675 nificant person.⁵¹ It's just improper, a lesson you could well have learned from the poisons of the Pharaohs, if you knew their history.

If you're anxious to be one of the wise, it's not enough just to change the rod into a serpent, you must be the great Aaron as well. I look for a complete transformation. And if you belong to the ranks of Egyptian magicians, be wholehearted in your practice of the art, if that's a good thing to do. No one is going to find fault with your expertise. However, if it's a bad thing, then stay away from it. And do spare my flock; because, for your information, however cleverly you play your part, you're depriving me of my one ewe lamb. What Nathan will denounce your counterfeit style? That sober garment of yours I shall rend if I get a chance: you have resort to it occasionally for a change just as one turns to coarser fare from satiety with finer foods. You, in turn, may rend a garment of mine, could anything be fairer? That is if you ever find me in the softer, meretricious kind. Yes, Laban must have the white garments;⁵² the stained ones are the portion of the shepherd who has labored much, who has shivered by night and been scorched by the day's heat. The most despicable trait of despicable people is the character they don; but be consistent in that character and I'm prepared to commend you.

Does the following anecdote have relevance in this context, by the way, how about it? One can, I dare say, in the midst of serious business indulge in some playful fancy—tears are diversified by laughter. The story goes⁵³ that a cat got into a bride's boudoir, and being all decked out in wedding garb she looked like a bride. There was a fine wedding, marriage gifts, rounds of applause, great fun. However, bride though she was, when the cat saw a mouse dart on the floor she pounced

---

51. Cf. Phaedrus, *Fabulae*, 1.24.1, "Inops potentem dum vult imitari perit" (When a man without resources tries to imitate the powerful he comes to grief.), B. E. Perry, ed., *Babrius*, Loeb, 218.

52. Cf. Gn 30.40.

53. For the story see *Babrii Fabulae Aesopeae*, 32, F. G. Schneidewin, ed., Teubner (Leipzig 1901), 15, and B. E. Perry, ed., *Babrius*, Loeb, 44–46.

on it, and instead of a wedding had supper. Your counterfeit teacher is always like that; he doesn't easily change his nature.

OBJECTION ANSWERED, 710-796

"But (someone objects) this man you're disparaging has an aptitude for affairs; judged either on old-fashioned methods or up-to-date manoeuvers he's a capable leader; whereas the other type of man may be saintly indeed, but he's useless to anyone but himself." Now that's a thoroughly wretched argument. No one, in fact, good, bad or indifferent, can be confined to himself alone. Just as air will absorb foul odors or fragrance, according to what it happens to encounter, so we too are molded by those about us, less intensely indeed by the good, but by the wicked a very great deal. Wickedness is much more readily imitated.

Now if our bishop happens to be a thorough scoundrel, we have an instance of the rod controlling the trees;[54] whereas if he's a man of high quality, once more great Israel, guided by the pillar of fire, makes its way toward the land of promise that everyone is seeking. The good bishop may not go about much, or be continually in the agora; or be a veritable Proteus[55] when it comes to adapting himself. He may not be a real Melampus[56] indeed, or any other model of versatility you like, in the ease of his adjustment to circumstances, whatever the sudden crisis happens to be. Can you reasonably describe as useless someone whose example is capable of improving us? Or describe as a good and efficient bishop someone whose example leads you to contempt for the men I praise? With really discerning people the overly impressive person does not find favor: what counts is genuine sincerity. However, you must have your model, and I mine. Now in the case of painting, do you regard as master, not people like

54. Cf. Jgs 9.15.
55. On Proteus see Homer, *Od.* 4.365.417-418.
56. On Melampus (*OCD*, [666]) who used the voices of birds and reptiles for divination, cf. Homer, *Od.* 11.287-297, 15.225-242.

Zeuxis, Polycleitus or Euphranor[57] who depict living figures with simple colors, but someone who uses florid and variegated hues to produce forms without vitality? Callimachus and Calais[58] were like that I think, in their labored attempts to give us images of images. So indeed is every flamboyant performer.

It is because of the standards you adopt that you have grown tired looking for a bishop. But your efforts have been so puny that I blush for them. You've been considering a bishop as you would an accountant, laying stress on mere rubbish, where I've been concerned with important issues. A priest should have one function and one only, the sanctification of souls by his life and teaching. He should raise them towards the heights by heavenly impulses. He should be serene, high-minded, reflecting like a mirror the godly and unspotted images that he has inside. For his flock he should send up holy offerings, until the day when he, too, shall perfect them into an offering. Other matters he should relinquish to those skilled in them. It is on such terms that our lives could become secure.

To be sure, you lay great stress on fearless speech; and for me, too, this is no small matter, provided that reason and common sense be observed. In actual fact the truth is this: a wise man's silence is more effective than all your eloquence; because in your case boldness is substituted for courage whereas, in his, native restraint makes for fewer words. However, should an occasion arise for really fearless speech, you will see the mild man transformed into a warrior and you will realize what a champion he can be. When your puny human efforts, weighted by the burden of a guilty conscience, meet with rejection while his blameless life wins him ready acceptance, you will understand the distinction between a monkey's

---

57. For Zeuxis, Polycleitus, and Euphranor see *OCD* [1147], [854], [417] respectively, and *Or.* 28.25, *De theologia*, SC 250.154.

58. For Callimachus and Calais see *OCD*, [194], [192] respectively. Calais and Zetes were mythological sons of Boreas who participated in the Argonaut expedition and, being winged, were often so depicted on Greek vases.

scream and a lion's roar. A man's character is the most persuasive thing of all.

Consequently, even in this domain, your paragon comes off second best. True, he occupies a prominent public position: he is regaled at tables not his own: he regards everyone else as parvenu in the very measure that he himself merits contempt. The big city is the one and only thing he can crow about; and that's the very place will bring you to a bad end, because miscreants are multiplied there. Whenever did a city ass seek to be of more consequence than a country one? To be sure, he lives in the city; but he is what he is.

What a senseless mess: we might as well have everything definitely arranged to suit the scoundrels, and ruination appointed for the decent people! Because when the course is smooth for the wicked while the blameless encounter trouble, a wise man has his wisdom taxed severely. In such a general chaos, with all values topsy-turvy, the best policy is to alter course, find security for one's brief allotment of days, and arrange a serene closure for old age.

CONCLUSION, 797–836

Accordingly, you may have your thrones and your dominions, if these be the values that hold first place for you. I bid you farewell, you may go on hurling invectives, parcelling out patriarchies. Let the whole universe give way before you, and one incumbency be exchanged for another, one man ejected and another elevated, if you enjoy that sort of thing.[59] On with the show. As for me, I propose to withdraw to God. It is for Him I live and breathe, to Him alone that I turn my gaze. Before I was born my mother promised me to Him, and to

---

59. Allusion to the intrigues about the sees of Antioch and Constantinople. For Gregory's antipathy to episcopal rivalries cf. D. F. Winslow, *The Dynamics of Salvation: A Study in Gregory of Nazianzus* (Cambridge, Ma. 1979), 10–21.

Him dangers and a fair vision in the night have united me.[60] To Him I shall offer in sacrifice the pure motions of the mind, conversing with Him, person to person, in so far as one can attain that state.

Such then, on behalf of decent people,[61] is my message for the miscreants. Should anyone take offense at my remarks they will have found their target. For you, my friends, my message will be delivered in a better place. At the moment I offer you a brief valediction, brief indeed, but from which you can profit. Please accept it in the spirit in which people receive their father's final words, advice worth remembering. The words sink all the deeper into memory, because after them one hears no more at all.

Should you, my friends, find another Gregory, be kinder to him.[62] Should you not, it only remains for you to be upright in dealings with your colleagues and yourselves; because your agreement has been proportionate only to the sway of the same ambitions among you. Cling always to the peace for which I strove, and lay aside those private failings by which the whole world is miserably confused. I shall for my part overlook the treatment I received. Who knows, perhaps I am wiser than others; perhaps my great age makes me irritable and morose; perhaps when a man is drunk all by himself all the sober ones seem drunk to him? Pass laws as you please, but be mindful of all I endured because my friends are what they are. My good sense indeed proved very helpful, and my great age provided the way out of troubles. When all this conflict which brings envy in its train is over, perhaps some friendly spirit[63] will bring about a peace.

60. Cf. *Carmina de seipso*, XLV.*De animae suae calamitatibus carmen lugubre*, PG 37.1370–1371, vv.233–259.
61. He probably has in mind the orthodox clergy and faithful.
62. Evidently Nectarius has not yet been elected.
63. *i.e.*, a new patriarch.

III CONCERNING HIS OWN LIFE
De vita sua II/I/XI*

---

*The text is found in Migne, PG 37.1029–1166. Christoph Jungck, ed., *Gregor von Nazianz: De Vita Sua* (Heidelberg 1974) has an introduction, commentary, text, and facing German translation. See also J. T. Cummings, "Towards a Critical Edition of the Carmen de vita sua of St. Gregory Nazianzen," *StPatr* VII(=TU 92): 52–59.

DEDICATION, 1–50

The idea of this composition is to set forth the tale of my calamities or, if you will, of my achievements. Some, I fancy, depending upon inclination, will tend to see it this way, some that. And inclination is not a very good standard to judge by. Verse-making, however, is pleasant as a medicine for low spirits and, by sugaring the pill of instruction for young people as well, it makes sermonizing enjoyable. The tale is addressed to you people who were my flock once upon a time, but are now another's: to those in orthodox communion, that is, in case there are some not genuine. Because when I'm silent everyone becomes well disposed.

Citizens of the famed orb of the universe, dwellers in what I call the second cosmos, girt round with the glory of land and sea: O newly-fashioned Rome,[1] seat of another order of patricians, city of Constantine, pillar of might: hear, gentlemen, the tale of one utterly strange to falsehood, a man who has endured a great deal in many ups and downs, and come as a consequence to deeper realization.

Everything has melted away, even with the passage of time the good. Little or nothing now is left. After a place has been churned up by heavy rains only pebbles are left behind. The plight of all those people who never, even originally, stood in the ranks of the good, is of course of no great moment. They were brutish and earthbound.[2] The dread and raging torrent is ourselves. Ours, I must say it with tears, is the disruptive force. We sit, not worthily on our high thrones, leaders of the people, teachers of virtue, whose task it is to nourish souls with heavenly food. But we ourselves are famine struck: we are physicians of sickness but corpses ourselves, reeking with

---

1. cf. Socrates, *Hist. Eccl.* 2.41, Sozomenus *Hist. Eccl.* 4.23.
2. cf. Plato, *Rep.* 9.586a.

numberless diseases. We are supposed to be guides over precipitous routes,³ but we have never travelled the routes and do not travel them now. To evade such guides is the briefest way and surest precept of salvation. Their very elevation is their impeachment. The sanctuary molds not their lives but their pretensions.

Let everyone now and in time to come listen to the reasons which led me to set these things down, as I am not one to turn rhapsode to no purpose. It will be necessary to describe fully my vicissitudes, even though the tale be long, lest any false accounts about me gain currency. Wicked people have a way of imputing causes to those who suffered for the evil they themselves have wrought. The idea is to prejudice things further by their falsehoods and turn accusation away from themselves. So much by way of preface.

CHILDHOOD AND EDUCATION, 51–111

My father was every inch a gentleman, an old man, simple in style, an example in his life, truly a second patriarch Abraham.⁴ He did not just seem noble, like people nowadays: he really was.⁵ Once indeed he had been astray; but latterly he had become a friend of Christ, then afterwards a pastor, the best of all pastors. My mother,⁶ to describe her in a word, was a fit mate for a man of such quality, and her worth was comparable. Of pious lineage, she was herself still more pious, a woman in body, yes; but in character she eclipsed any man. For the virtue of their lives both parents were equally a by-

---

3. cf. Mt 15.14.
4. cf. *Or.* 8, *In laudem sororis Gorgoniae*, PG 35.794, FOTC 22.103(4): "Who is there who does not know our new Abraham and the Sara of our time? I mean Gregory and his wife Nonna?" See also *Epitaphia* 51–52, *Anth. Pal.*, 422–424.
5. cf. Plato, *Rep.*2.361b, quoting Aeschylus. This is repeated at v.321.
6. cf. *Or.* 8, *In laudem sororis Gorgoniae*, PG 35.793–796, FOTC 22.103(5): "This good shepherd was the product of his wife's prayers and guidance, and it was she who taught him the ideal of a good shepherd's conduct. . . . He is the ornament of men, she of women, and not only an ornament but also a pattern of virtue."

word. Can I demonstrate that, provide evidence? As witness
of the claim I shall adduce my mother herself, the very mouth
of truth. She was the kind who would sooner conceal some- 65
thing quite public than boast about private matters for vain-
glory. Fear was her guide: it is a good teacher.

She[7] was anxious to see a male child in her house: that is
indeed a wish common to many people. She turned to God 70
and prayed for the fulfilment of her wish,[8] for when her mind
was set on something she was not easily restrained. God
granted the favor, and in her great desire, failing not in loving
prayer, she actually anticipated it. There came to her a gra- 75
cious foretaste, a vision[9] containing the shadow of her re-
quest. My likeness and my name appeared clearly to her, the
work of a dream by night. Then I was born to them, the gift 80
of God the giver if worthy of the prayer: if not, it was because
of my own shortcomings.

So I came into this life formed, poor wretch, of clay and
compound elements, the elements which control us, or which
we with difficulty control. Yet I take this very birth as pledge 85
of all that's fairest, ingratitude is wrong. As soon as I made
my appearance, straightway in the noblest of contracts I be-
came Another's. Like some lamb, some pleasing calf, but a 90
victim of high quality endowed with reason I was offered to
God (I hesitate to say it) like a young Samuel.[10] But I am con-
sidering chiefly the sentiments of those who offered me. Be-
cause from earliest infancy I was nurtured in all virtue, hav-
ing as I had the best example in my home.

Already I was taking on some of the dignity of age, and 95
little by little, like a cloud from out a cloud, desire for better

---

7. On Nonna see Dölger, *Antike und Christentum* 5 (1936): 44–75.
8. Cf. 1 Kgs 1.10ff. For further details on his mother see *Or.* 18.7–12, *Funebris in patrem*, PG 35.992–1000, FOTC 22.124–128(8–12), *Epitaphia* 24–74, *Anth. Pal.*, 410–430.
9. Nonna's dream is described in *Carmina de seipso*, I.*De rebus suis*, PG 37.1002, vv.429ff, and XLV.*De animae suae calamitatibus carmen lugubre*, PG 37.1369, vv.229ff, and *Or.* 18, *Funebris in patrem*, PG 35.1021–1024, FOTC 22.144(30).
10. Cf. 1 Kgs 1.20, quoted in *Or.* 43, *Funebris oratio in laudem Basilii Magni Caesareae in Cappadocia episcopi*, PG 36.596, FOTC 22.91(73).

things led me on. As reason developed I forged onwards. Of
books I enjoyed those that led to God: of men I associated
with those excellent in character.

So was it with me in these matters. In the narration of other
matters I am at a loss about the proper course to take. Am I
to hide the wonders by means of which God led me on, molding the good promise my eagerness displayed? For thus does
He lead us to salvation? Or am I to speak out boldly and publish what occurred? One course seems ungrateful, the other
not devoid of pride. Better to be silent, it is enough for me to
know. My present state, which falls so sadly short of my fervor
at that time, might seem too much at variance. Just what is
necessary then I shall make known publicly.

DEPARTURE FOR ATHENS, 112–121

When the first down grew on my cheeks a keen passion for
letters took possession of me. Moreover I sought to turn bastard letters into the service of those that are genuine; because
I did not want people who have learned absolutely nothing
but vain and empty dexterity of tongue, which consists of
lungs and loudness, to preen themselves. And I did not wish
to get tied up in the intricacies of sophisms. Allowing anything to take precedence over my Christian studies never entered my mind.

SHIPWRECK, 121–209

The usual tendency of youthful spirits however, a readiness
to be swayed by chaotic impulses, this I did experience, just
like a spirited colt who plunges for the race. I had been getting some smattering of letters at Alexandria,[11] and the moment I chose to leave was altogether outside the sailing season, before the sea had settled down. People skilled in such

11. On studying letters at Alexandria cf. P. Gallay, *La vie*, 34ff.

matters point out that there is a dangerous tail of Taurus[12] at this time and that seafaring is a matter of hardihood not good sense. I put off and was making straight for Greece in the lee of Cyprus, when the ship was struck by a squall.[13] Everything became a great blackness: land, sea, air, the sky all darkened. Thunderclaps resounded amid flashes of lightning, and the sheets quivered as the sails were filled. The mainmast bent: the rudder had no effect as the blasts tore it forcibly from one's hands. Mountainous seas swamped the vessel. A confused clamor arose, cries of sailors, helmsmen, officers, passengers, all calling with one voice upon Christ, even the people who formerly knew not God. Fear is an opportune teacher. The most pitiable of all our misfortunes, however, was that the boat was without water. The moment she began to roll, the cistern which carried the precious treasure of water was smashed and scattered to the depths. The question then was whether thirst, or the sea, or the winds should make an end of us. But God sent speedy deliverance from it all. Phoenician merchants suddenly made their appearance. They were in fear themselves; but when they realized from our entreaties how desperate our plight was, they made our craft fast by using grappling hooks and main strength, for they were very strong. They rescued us indeed from a state of practical shipwreck, like fish gasping out of native element, or a lamp flickering out when all the oil is gone.[14]

The sea continued angry, however, and we were harassed for several days. Driven hither and thither we had no notion of where we were sailing, and we could see no hope of safety from God. All of us feared a common death, but more terrifying for me was the hidden death. Those murderous waters

12. On the "tail of Taurus" cf. *Carmina de seipso*, I.*De rebus suis*, PG 37.993, vv.308–321. See also Jungck's learned astronomical note on v.126 for the precise date of sailing. The storm is also described in *Or.* 18, *Funebris in patrem*, PG 35.1024, FOTC 22.144–145(31).
13. This famous description of a storm (vv.130–209) has been translated by H. S. Boyd, *Select Poems of Synesius and Gregory Nazianzen* (London 1814), 14–18, and reproduced in part in G. Misch, *History of Autobiography*, 2.602.
14. He returns to the lamp image at v.600, and again in *Carmina de seipso*, I.*De rebus suis*, PG 37.1011, vv.550–555.

were keeping me away from the purifying waters which divinize us. That was *my* lament and *my* misfortune. For this I kept sending up cries and stretching out my hands, and my cries overcame the pounding of the waves. Stretched miserable and prone I lay with garments rent. It seems unbelievable, but it is perfectly true, that all forgot their own particular woes and joined their prayerful entreaties to mine. The way in which they shared my agonies proclaimed them pious fellows, voyagers on a common sea of woe.

However thou, my Christ, wert even then a mighty saviour, just as now thou art my deliverer from the storms of life. There was no shred of solid hope, no island, no mainland, no mountain top, no beacon light, no guiding star for sailors: nothing large or small that one could see.

What was I to do? Was there any way out of the hazards? Despairing of all hope here below, I turned to thee, my life, my breath, my light, my strength, my salvation, the source of terror and affliction, but the benign healer too, ever weaving good into the dark pattern. I reminded thee of all the miracles of time past when we had experience of thy mighty hand: of the sea sundered and the passage of Israel; of enemies defeated by hands raised in prayer; of the affliction by scourges of the Egyptians with their leaders;[15] of the reduction to servitude of creation; of walls collapsing at the sound of the trumpet[16] and the people's onset. My entreaties were added to all the famous pleas of old.

Thine, I said, I have been formerly, thine am I now. Please accept me for a second time, the possession of thy honored servants, the gift of land and sea, dedicated by the prayers of my mother and by this unparalleled crisis. If I escape a double danger[17] I shall live for thee, if I am abandoned, thou wilt lose a worshipper. At this moment thy disciple is tossed upon the wave. For my sake dispel slumber, wake to me and let the fear be stilled.[18]

---

15. Ex 7, 14.2, 17.11.   16. Jos 6.
17. "double danger," *i.e.*, physical shipwreck and spiritual death before baptism.
18. Cf. Mk 6.48.

These were my words. The clash of winds abated, the sea grew calm, the ship sailed straight on course—all the result of my prayer. The whole ship's company went their way praising the great Christ, for they had received a double salvation at the hands of God. We passed Rhodes and a little later struck sail in the harbor of Aegina, for it was an Aeginetan craft.

AT ATHENS, 210–264

Subsequently came Athens and letters.[19] I leave to others the account of what transpired there, how, realizing that first things are first, I walked in the fear of God. Even though in the bloom of youth and on the wave of adventure students find themselves sucked headlong into one gang or another,[20] I kept a quiet tenor. I dare say, as the belief goes, a spring in the sea is sweet by contrast with the brackish waters.[21] I was not attracted by people who fell on deleterious paths: on the contrary, I myself led friends towards better things. Here, too, God favored me. He associated with me the very wisest person, one towering above all others in learning and in life. You will very easily identify the man I mean.

Basil, of course, it was, the great ornament of our generation. In studies, in lodgings, in discussions I had him as companion. We made a team, if I may boast a little, that was celebrated throughout Greece. We had all things in common, and a single soul, as it were, bound together our two distinct bodies. But above all it was God, of course, and a mutual desire for higher things, that drew us to each other. As a result

19. For a translation of vv.211ff. see J. H. Newman, *Historical Sketches* (London 1894), 2.52–53. Gregory further describes the Athens days in his *Or*.43, *Funebris oratio in laudem Basilii Magni Caesareae in Cappadocia episcopi*, PG 36.513–516, FOTC 22.38–40(14–15).

20. For fuller details about student gangs, initiation, etc., cf. *Or.* 43, *Funebris oratio in laudem Basilii Magni Caesareae in Cappadocia episcopi*, PG 36.513–517, FOTC 22.39–40(15–16).

21. The thought recurs in *Or*.43, *Funebris oratio in laudem Basilii Magni Caesareae in Cappadocia episcopi*, PG 36.524, FOTC 22.45(21).

we reached such a pitch of confidence that we revealed the depths of our hearts, becoming ever more united in our yearning. There is no such solid bond of union as thinking the same thoughts.

There remained the future—homecoming, and a way of life. Our studies took a great deal of time, already I was practically in my thirtieth year. Then I came to realize in what affection and regard our fellow students held us, for the moment of departure had come, and with it great pain. It was the occasion for embraces, for those hateful words of farewell, and for exhortations to remember. Basil set forth the reasons for going away, and people were persuaded only with great difficulty. But they yielded all the same. Even at this moment, when I recall the throngs around us then, my tears begin to flow.

Suddenly I was encircled by everyone, strangers, friends, fellow students and teachers. Affection drove them to such lengths that they mingled a little pressure with protestations and laments. They held on to me tightly, insisting that they would not let me go for any reason. It was not right that venerable Athens should lose me, to whom they were prepared to concede by vote the primacy of letters. They finally prevailed upon me, for only an oak tree could withstand such laments and entreaties.

Not fully however, for my native land was beckoning, that country which in orthodoxy surpasses practically all under the sun. It seemed a noble ideal to live the philosophic life there and as time passed my aged parents were sinking. Accordingly for another little while I lingered at Athens. Then almost by stealth I slipped away.

HOME AGAIN, CHOICE OF LIFE, 265–336

When I arrived home, to satisfy the inordinate desire of some people who kept importuning me, I gave a display of eloquence. It was, so to speak, a debt I owed because personally I place no value upon vapid applause, or upon those stupid and intricate conceits which are the delight of sophists when a crowd of youth confronts them. The first step in my concept of the philosophic life had long been this: to sacrifice to God as well as everything else the labor of letters too, like people who abandon their property to be grazed by sheep, or cast the treasure they have amassed to the bottom of the sea. However, as I said, for my friends I gave a performance.

But these were like mere training bouts, a preliminary initiation for the greater mysteries. Manly undertakings would be called for in the future. Privately I had recourse to the judgment of friends who were genuine advisers in my thinking.

My mind was in fact in the throes of an intense brainstorm, because I was in search of the noblest among noble purposes.[22] I had long previously made up my mind to reject the flesh completely, and now the idea pleased me more. But as I surveyed the actual paths to holiness it was not easy to discern the better path or the serene one. As often happens in the practical domain, for different reasons this course or that seemed good or bad. My state can best be illustrated by an example. A man is planning a long journey, but he quails before the voyage and the hardships of the sea. I was for travelling the road that presented least difficulty.

Elias the Thesbite would come into my mind, or the great Carmel, or that strange food the Precursor had, or the austere life of the sons of Jonadab.[23] Then again the love of the sacred books would dominate me, the light of the Spirit in contemplation of the Word: this was not work suitable for the detachment of the desert. Finally, after hesitating considerably between the two courses, I came to this solution, for conflicting desires had brought my mental turmoil to a reasonable calm.

I kept noticing that those who are attracted by an active life do good to some of the people they encounter. But they do

22. For a verse translation of vv.280–315 see J. H. Newman, *Historical Sketches*, 56–57, reproduced in G. Misch, *History of Autobiography*, 2.603–604.
23. Cf. 1 Kgs 18.42 (Elias); Jer 35.6ff. (sons of Jonadab); Mt 3.1 (John the Baptist).

themselves no good and are harassed by anxieties that wreck their serenity. On the other hand, those that stay detached are somehow more stable and turn with quiet mind to God. But their charity is narrow, they are useful only to themselves, the life they live is unsocial and harsh.

I decided upon a middle way[24] between the life without ties and the life of mixing, one which would combine the serenity of the former with the practical use of the latter.

There was moreover a stronger consideration, the matter of courtesy to those worthy folk (my parents I mean) to whom I owed a debt. I was concerned about their old age; for it is a very pious duty to give prime respect, after God, to one's parents. They are responsible for our very knowledge of God. I supported them with all my strength, I led them by the hand, so that by showing consideration for old age I might make provision for my own old age; because as we sow we reap.

Part of my philosophy was this: not just to *seem* concerned about the higher life, to *be* rather than to seem a friend of God. Consequently I took the view that people living the active life, too, deserve our love. They receive their measure of honor from God because they lead people by means of the divine mysteries. Still, however much I seemed involved with people, I was possessed by a greater longing for monastic life, which I regarded as a matter of interior dispositions, not of physical situation. For the sanctuary I had reverence, but from a good distance, the effect being that of sunlight upon weak eyes. In all the ups and downs of life I had hoped for any other dignity than this. In sum, one can say nothing ambitious when one is mere man: envy always goes with elevation. And one need seek no other evidence than my own experience.

ORDINATION, 337–437

While in this frame of mind I became involved in a serious crisis. My father was well aware of my thinking. Nevertheless

---

24. For Gregory's "middle way" cf. T. Špidlík, "La theoria et la praxis chez Grégoire de Nazianze," *StPatr* XIV(=TU 117): 358–364, esp. 360.

he exerted pressure to raise me to an auxiliary throne, so that
he might constrain me by the bonds of the Spirit and pay me
the highest honor in his power. Why he did so I cannot say.
Perhaps he was moved by fatherly affection, which when combined with power is a considerable force. Tyranny of this kind
(I can call it by no other name and may the Holy Spirit pardon
me for feeling thus)²⁵ so distressed me that I suddenly shook
myself free of everyone, friends, parents, fatherland, kin.
Like an ox stricken by the gadfly I made for Pontus, anxious
to have the most godly of my friends as medicine for my agitation. For there, hidden in that cloud, like one of the sages
of old,²⁶ practising union with God, was Basil, who is now with
the angels. With him I soothed my agony of spirit.

But when my good father, under stress of years and yearning, kept beseeching his son to respect his last gasps, I hastened into the abyss once more,²⁷ something I should never
have done. It was a crisis that saddled me with misfortune. I
feared the reproach of an aged parent, lest the affection between us should issue for me in a curse; because simplicity,
when angered, is capable of this.

Then after a short interval the storm broke once more with
an intensity that is indescribable indeed, except that divulging
all to friends is a help.

My brother²⁸ held at the time the secular office of treasurer.
O wicked one, what power you do have! He died in the middle
of his term and a horde of miscreants descended upon what
remained of his estate. Household servants, strangers, friends
began to plunder everything—everyone goes hunting when
an oak falls. From my point of view, being as I am a bird easily
borne aloft, mundane business would have caused no great
anxiety. But I was obliged to suffer through with everyone,

---

25. Cf. *Or.* 2, *Apologeticus de fuga*, SC 247.84–240. On "tyranny" cf. SC 247.96 n.2.
26. *i.e.*, Moses.
27. This was the occasion for *Or.* 1, *In sanctum Pascha et in tarditatem*, PG 35.396–401, SC 247.72–83.
28. *i.e.*, Caesarius, cf. *Epitaphia* 88–100, *Anth. Pal.*, 438–444, *Or.* 7, *Funebris in laudem Caesarii fratris oratio*, PG 35.756ff. See also A. H. M. Jones, et al., *Prosopography*, 169–170.

good and bad, by the side of my good father, sharing with him the trouble, that is, not the property. People who once had a firm footing, when they slip, are no longer able to help themselves, and fall down the cliff. So it was with me. Once I got a taste of trouble, disaster followed disaster. Basil, the closest of our friends, came to visit us. (I should like to pass over intervening events in silence, lest I seem to speak in insulting terms about a man whose eulogy I've just pronounced.)[29] He came, alas for the story, but I must tell it all the same. He was to prove another father to me, and a far more burdensome one. My real father, even though he tyrannized over me, I must shelter; but no such duty holds in his case, where friendship actually brought injury instead of deliverance from trouble. I cannot know whether I should lay more blame on my own sins, which often indeed have tortured me (the incident is always fresh and rankling in my mind), or on the highhanded style you acquired with the throne, O best of men.[30]

In other respects, such as the studies we pursued together, you yourself would be slow to claim superiority. Nor, sir, did you in former times ever make such a claim; and had you done so, some wise observer who knew us both well would have restrained you. What came over you? How was it that you so suddenly cast me off? Any style of friendship that so deals with friends should perish from the earth. We were lions yesterday, and today I am an ape. But of course even a lion is trifling in your eyes. And even if you took this view of your friends generally (I shall say the conceited thing) I did not deserve this, the man you set above your friends. That was before you climbed so high you thought everything beneath you. But what is the point of chafing, O my spirit. Curb the steed by force.[31]

---

29. The eulogy on Basil (*Or.*43, *Funebris oratio in laudem Basilii Magni Caesareae in Cappadocia episcopi*) was preached at Caesarea on January 1, 382. These verses must have been written immediately afterwards. On *Or.* 43 see G. Kennedy, *Greek Rhetoric*, 228–237.

30. For his rancor with Basil cf. *Or.* 43, *Funebris oratio in laudem Basilii Magni Caesareae in Cappadocia episcopi*, PG 36.580.

31. For his fondness for metaphors from horse-riding cf. *Or.* 43, *Funebris oratio in laudem Basilii Magni Caesareae in Cappadocia episcopi*, PG 36.525,

Again my narrative turns towards its goal. In other respects the soul of integrity, that man was falsity itself to me. He had often heard me say that the situation, even if it worsened, could be endured for the present; but that, should my parents die, I was altogether for leaving mundane affairs. I wanted to reap some benefit from a life without ties, feeling ready as I did to be a citizen of any place. Though he knew this and had voiced approval of it, nevertheless he was the one who forced me to the bishop's throne, he and my father, who was dealing me a second blow. Be patient and listen to the total story. Had my enemies deliberated long about a means to dishonor me, I don't think they would have found a better one than this. If you wish to hear about it you can hear from all those people who thought it an unfair proceeding. Pontus knows, and the city of Caesarea, and all our mutual friends, how I conducted myself in regard to my friend. It would be small of me to cast that up, the person who has received kindnesses should remember them, not the one who did them. Let the facts demonstrate how *he* treated me.

CONSECRATION AS BISHOP OF SASIMA, 440–517

Midway along the high road through Cappadocia,[32] where the road divides into three, there's a stopping place. It's without water or vegetation, not quite civilized, a thoroughly deplorable and cramped little village. There's dust all around the place, the din of wagons, laments, groans, tax officials, implements of torture, and public stocks. The population consists of casuals and vagrants. Such was my church of Sasima. He who was surrounded by fifty *chorepiscopi* was so mag-

---

FOTC 22.45–46(22), NPNF, ser. 2, 7.403, and *Or.* 45.10, *In sancta Pascha*, PG 36.636, NPNF, ser. 2, 7.426.

32. For the Sasima incident in 372, cf. S. Giet, *Sasimes, une méprise de S. Basile* (Paris 1941), *Or.* 9, *Apologeticus ad patrem*, PG 35.820–825, *Or.* 10, *In seipsum ad patrem et Basilium magnum*, PG 35.828–832, *Or.*11, *Ad Gregorium Nyssenum*, PG 35.832–841, B. Gain, *L' Église de Cappadoce au IVe siècle d'après la correspondance de Basile de Césarée (330–379)* (Roma 1985), 308–309, esp. 308 n.89, P. Gallay, *La vie*, 109–112.

nanimous as to make me incumbent here. The whole idea was to get the better of a violent intruder by founding a new see. And among his warrior friends apparently I held first place. O yes, I was an able fighter once, wounds that are blessed being no great disaster. For, added to the features I've already enumerated, that particular see couldn't be held without bloodshed. It was a no man's land between two rival bishops. A division of our native province, which set up two metropolises for the small towns, gave occasion for the outbreak of a fearful brawl. The pretext was souls; but in fact, of course, it was desire for control, control (I hesitate to say it) of taxes and contributions, which have the whole world in a miserable commotion.

In the name of God where did the proper course of action lie for me? Acquiescence? Patient endurance of assaults by scoundrels? Blows at all hours? Suffocation by dust? Not to have a place to rest my aging bones? Always being driven forcibly from my house? Not having bread to break with a guest? Penniless, with a penniless flock for my portion, unable to discover anywhere a corrective for the evils with which cities are filled? Feeding upon thorns with never a rose[33] to cull, always a harvest of trouble without a single redeeming feature? Offer this sort of thing, if you please, to people with more wisdom than I can muster, and request another sort of generosity from me. Athens, our studies together, our sharing of roof and hearth, the single spirit animating two people, the marvel of Greece, the pledge that we made that we would cast aside absolutely the world and live the coenobitic life for God, placing our words in the service of the one wise Word! This was the outcome of it all! Everything was shattered, abandoned on the ground, the old high hopes were gone with the wind. Where was one to turn? Wild beasts, will you not receive me? For you, in my view at least, have greater loyalty. Such, in brief compass, was that particular situation.

Bent as now I am, not in mind but in body, what words can

---

33. Cf. F. W. Norris, "Of Thorns and Roses: The Logic of Belief in Gregory Nazianzen," *ChH* 53 (1984): 455–464.

I find? How to set forth my agony for you in its entirety? Once more the goad struck me: I became a fugitive again, making for the mountain³⁴ in search of my pet luxury, that beloved mode of life. Little gain I had—I cannot be, it seems, a very good fugitive. Though schooled to bear all things, this one weakness I do have, that I cannot bear my father's wrath. To begin with, he made a determined effort to settle me in Sasima. But then, as his health worsened, he adopted a second line. I ought not to remain in the inferior position; I should become his auxiliary (by this stage he was much afflicted physically) and lighten his labors. He entreated me with outstretched hands, and touched my beard, with words to this effect:³⁵

"Dearest of sons, your father implores you. The aged father turns to the young man, the master to the servant, servant by nature and by double law. My child, I am not asking you for gold, or precious stones, or silver, or estates, or any material goods. I am asking you to set yourself beside Aaron and Samuel³⁶ and become an honored minister of God. You are in the arms of the man who begat you. As you hope to find the one and only Father merciful to you, do not, my child, rebuff me. The favor I ask is a good thing and, even if it were not, it is a father's request.³⁷ Your span of life does not yet measure the length of my sacrificial ministry. Let me have this favor, or let some other hand lay me in the grave. That is the punishment I determine if you disobey. The few short days that remain let me have; dispose, as you please, of what comes afterwards."

---

34. See B. Otis, "The Throne and the Mountain," *CJ* 56 (1961): 146–165.
35. The speech assigned to his father (vv.502–517) is a good example of prosopopoiia.
36. For Samuel cf. *Epitaphia* 27, *Anth. Pal.*, 412.
37. On his father's request cf. *Epitaphia* 21–22, 75–76, *Anth. Pal.*, 410, 432.

RETURN TO NAZIANZUS, 518–561

My spirit shook off depression to some extent on hearing this, like the sun a cloud. What then? What outcome had my troubles? I took myself to task. So far as his see was concerned, there could be no harm in acceding to my father's wish. It will not hold me, I argued, against my will, for I am bound neither by decree nor promise. And so parental fear won the day and brought me back again. Then, when my parents passed away to receive the reward they had so long been seeking, I was left alone. I was not quite a free agent. On the one hand, I had not touched at all the church allotted to me, even to the extent of offering a single sacrifice there, or leading the congregation in prayer, or ordaining a single cleric. But, on the other hand, I cannot deny that for some short time, like an outsider with something not his own, I did exercise a sort of ministry in our native church. People would not let me go. Oaths were sworn. Some pious folk brought pressure to bear, with information about intrigues by a group of reprobates.

All the time I kept telling the bishops about the situation, begging them from the bottom of my heart to appoint some bishop to the town. Two points I kept making with absolute truth: that I had not been allotted any church by formal decree, and secondly that I had long made up my mind to get away from friends and from mundane affairs.

But I failed to persuade them. Some wanted me to go on ruling because of their regard for me: others were perhaps on the high and mighty side. Consequently I fled in the first instance to Seleucia to the convent of the holy virgin Thecla.[38] My feeling was that they would tire of the delay and quickly decide to put someone in charge. Here quite a considerable time elapsed. But I got involved again in troubles and found none of the advantages I had expected. On the contrary, as though it were destined to be so, a great array of the very affairs I had thought to escape loomed up.

38. On Thecla see *Or.* 21, *In laudem Athanasii*, PG 35.1081–1128, NPNF, ser. 2, 7.275.

At this point I shall merely summarize the narrative. It is for people who know the story well; but I want them to have it (since they no longer have me) as balm for their wounds. To my enemies, I want it to be a reproach and, to my friends, a testimony of the extent to which I who had wronged nobody was myself wronged.

CONSTANTINOPLE, 562–664

Nature has not given us two suns; but she gave us two Romes, an old and a new, to stand as beacon lights for the whole universe. The only difference between them is that one lights the East and the other the West, but with complementary and harmonious brilliance. However, in the matter of the faith, the course of one has for a considerable time run smoothly, and it still does. As befits the primal see she binds the whole West to the word of salvation, worshipping the total symphony of God. The course of the other was previously upright; but now it no longer is. I speak of my own city (or rather, not mine now, of course).

It has lain in the abyss of destruction ever since Alexandria, that shallow, empty town, gave Arius,[39] the abomination of desolation, to the world. He was the first who said "the Trinity is not to be worshipped." He set limits of dignity for the single nature, clumsily divided the indivisible essence, and scattered us in splintered groups along diverse paths.

The hapless city, it is true, was in bad case; for custom, backed by time, issues as law, and it had been brought through infidelity to death's door by the law of time. Nevertheless some slight spark of life-giving breath remained. There were souls perfect in the word of faith, a tiny group indeed, but larger in the sight of God. He does not reckon numbers but hearts, and these were a faithful growth, a branch deserving honor. As God would have it, (for people thought me prominent in career and eloquence, though I had always lived a

39. On Arius cf. SC 250.25–28.

595 provincial life) at the instance of many pastors and their flocks, the grace of the Spirit sent me to these as helper for the people and support of orthodoxy. Parched souls that were
600 still verdant would be refreshed by a pious inflow; and the light still burning in the lamp[40] would be nourished by absorbing oil. Solid teaching would break down or dissipate the undisciplined tongues and involved word-weavings which
605 drain the simplicity out of faith, those spiders' webs and ghastly traps which the strong ridicule, but in which the simple get enmeshed. And those who had got caught in the toils would escape.

AS CHAMPION OF ORTHODOXY HE CONFRONTS APOLLINARISM, 609–630

And so I came as the champion of orthodoxy, not of my own will, but overborne by pressure from people. There
610 was some talk about a group of bishops whose teaching, a newfangled heresy,[41] was being introduced into friendly churches. It gave a truncated version of the manner in which the Logos of God was joined to humanity. He actually entered this union without distortion, taking upon Himself man, com-
615 plete with *psyche, nous,* a body capable of suffering, the whole of the first Adam, that is, except sin. But they introduced the notion of God without *nous,* through fear apparently that the concepts were irreconcilable. I should be more inclined to fear precisely this about the nature of flesh (*sarx*), for it is an
620 element far more removed from God. Or else they had decided that whereas other elements of human nature needed redemption, *nous* was utterly lost. Actually it, more than any element, had to be saved by God, for in the case of Adam it,

---

40. For the lamp image cf. n.14, *supra*.
41. The new-fangled heresy is Apollinarism. See E. Mühlenberg, "Apollinaris," *TRE* 3.362–371. See also M. Aubineau, ch.VII "In Centurionem et contra Manichaeos et Apollinaristas" in *Un Traité Inédit de Christologie de Sévérien de Gabala,* Cahiers d'Orientalisme V (Genève 1983), and E. Mühlenberg, *Apollinaris von Laodicea* (Göttingen 1969) 46: 50–58.

above all, was what fell. In his *nous* he received the command, in his *nous* he transgressed it. The transgressing element must be the assumed element as well. I cannot have it that I, who have been impaired in my whole nature, should be saved only partially by the Word. I will not have God dishonored by the suggestion that He did not fully assume my nature, but only the element of clay. On their showing, all that has been saved is the *nous*-less *psyche* of a brute.

HE ALSO OPPOSES ARIANISM, 631–664

Every religious person should abandon such ideas. From the opposite angle a similar error is made by people who put forward the ill-considered theory of two sons, one of God and one of the virgin. Both groups destroy the essential proportion of the Incarnation, the first by wiping out something, the second by doubling it. If we accept the idea of two sons I fear we are confronted by a dilemma. We must either worship two gods instead of one, or while guarding against this error we must exclude anything synthetic from God.[42] For God could never experience any fleshly thing. Now actually the Incarnation meant complete merging of human nature with the whole God. It was not like the case of a prophet or any other inspired person, where there is not a participation in God but in divine qualities. Here there was a blending of essences as between sun and rays. There is then no room for discussion with people who refuse to worship the Man-God as unique, the assumer with the assumed, the timeless and Him who became involved in time, Son of the only Father and the only mother, the two natures blended in the one Christ.

But to return to my affairs, how did things stand? When I arrived I became involved in many troubles. To begin with, the city was up in arms against me for introducing several gods instead of one. It was no wonder really. Previous lead-

---

42. Cf. Col 2.9. On Arianism see A. M. Ritter, "Arianismus," *TRE* 3.692–719, esp. 713ff., *Or.* 31.7, *De spiritu sancto*, SC 250.286

ership had left the people altogether ignorant of orthodox truth, how the One was triune and the Trinity in turn One, given a theological understanding of both. Furthermore a mob tends to side with someone who is challenged; and quite a large public, filled with excitement, rallied to the person who was at the time their champion and pastor. He had their pity as salve for his wounds, for in the eyes of these people defeat in any matter was the ultimate disgrace.

INITIAL TROUBLES, 665–735

The stonings (my particular paradise) I forbear to mention. Indeed I've only one criticism. The aim was poor, finding the sort of target which makes a hollow mockery of success. Then I was brought before the magistrate as a murderer: I, a disciple of the Word, who had never perpetrated, or meditated, an untoward action in my life. These gentlemen follow a noble and elevated policy, the sole principle of which is to avoid alienating popular sentiment. But there stood by my side Christ, with His sustaining counsel, as champion of my teaching. It is He who knows how to deliver strangers from lions, to turn fire into dew for the refreshment of young men, to make of a whale the oratory of the pious. At that court of the stranger it was He who glorified me.

At this stage an intense dissension flared up in my group. I was being torn between Paul and Apollo.[43] They never became incarnate for me, or showed their blood in memorable sufferings, and am I to be named after them, not after the Savior? The opposition created confusion and turbulence everywhere, maintaining that the church if left alone was in excellent case. But when a harmful element tilts the balance against discipline, how can there be stability in a ship, a city, an army, a troupe of dancers, a household?

Such was the plight of the flock of Christ in those days.

43. Cf. 1 Cor 1.12ff.

Before they could achieve any maturity or independence, before they were delivered indeed from the swaddling clothes of infancy or could walk securely, this splendid offspring were set upon by wolves in the sight of their father, were scattered and sundered. The wolves bore down upon me ravenously in my childless state. Poverty-stricken wretch that I was, wrinkled and bowed and shabby, wasted by fasting and by tears for fear of the future, the reprehensible object of their cruelties, a stranger and a wanderer, hidden in the bowels of the earth, they could not endure that I should have more influence than the vigorous and the strong.

One could sense their thinking: "We are flatterers, you are not. We revere thrones, you, holiness. We love luxury, you simplicity. You eat the salt of nourishment, but you spurn the seasoning of delicacies. We are the slaves of opportunity and of the people's whim, we always veer the craft with whatever wind blows. Like the chameleon and the polypus we're always changing the color of our language. But you, in your impudence, are as unyielding as an anvil. On the principle that the faith has always been one, you limit the teaching of truth to overnarrow confines, invariably following the limited trail of Scripture. How is it, sir, that you draw the people with your chattering tongue and direct well aimed shafts against the shoddy thinking of members of variegated sects? You've one side for your friends, another for outsiders: a magnet in one instance, a dangerous adversary in the other."

"Well, if there be nothing wrong in this, and there is not, why complain as if it were extraordinary? And if there is something wrong which only you can perceive, then give a fair judgment as a minister of God. Destroy me, the guilty party, but let the people go. Their only crime is support of myself and being influenced by my teaching."

Though a bit daunted by the unusual experience, initially I was able to cope with things. The effect was that of a sudden din upon the ears or a sudden flash of lightning when one is inexperienced. But at that time I was unimpaired and had the strength to bear anything. And furthermore I had good

hope that once extricated from practical affairs I would not
get similarly involved in the future. This encouraged me to
endure the unpleasantness more equably.

THE EPISODE OF MAXIMUS, THE CYNIC PHILOSOPHER, 736–830[44]

When we get to the troubles that came my way subsequently, however, their very narration leaves me at a loss. O wicked demon, purveyor of woe, where did you get the power to contrive so great a wrong? It was not blood, or frogs, or gnats, or flies, or pestilence of flocks, or boils, or hail, or locusts, or darkness, or (the last plague)[45] the destruction of the firstborn, that afflicted me, and plunged the people under the Red Sea's wave. These were the celebrated plagues of the fierce Egyptians: no, what ousted me was Egyptian fickleness, and how it happened is worth hearing. May this account forever commemorate the performance.

At that time the city harbored an Egyptian freak. He was of dubious sex, a raging pest, a dog, a cynic, a street-lounger, an Ares,[46] an inarticulate nuisance, a colossal monster. Fair? dark? curly? straight-haired? He had been one way, then recently he had contrived to be the other—the coiffeur's art could do him all over again. Plaiting the philosopher's coil of golden hair is mostly a woman's art, but it has become the male province, too.

Why shouldn't wise men have these feminine cosmetics on their faces?[47] There's little point in restricting such ugly and disgusting adornments to wise women only—it's a mute indication of the character beneath. As if men can't have their

---

44. On Maximus cf. J. Mossay, AnBoll 100 (1982): 229–236, J. Bernardi, *La Prédication*, 168–181.
45. For the plagues cf. Ex 8.
46. On Ares, cf. Homer, *Od*.8.266–366.
47. Gregory's antipathy to feminine cosmetics is dwelt on at length in *Carmina Moralia* 29, *Adversus mulieres se nimis ornantes*, PG 37.884–908. See the edition by A. Knecht, *Gregorius Nazianzus: Gegen die Putzsucht der Frauen* (Heidelberg 1972).

Maximuses too! The fact indeed was pointed up by his hair style. It had previously managed to escape notice, we had to wait for contemporary philosophers to provide such marvels. To be ambiguous, that is, in nature and configuration, one must have a share of either sex, a woman in hair style, and a man by reason of the staff. He used to preen himself and thought himself a person of consequence in the city. He always had the endearing curls falling about his shoulders and despatched his brilliant sallies from the mane of hair. His culture was all concentrated in his *ensemble*.

Rumor has it that this gentleman had come by many questionable routes which, in particular, I let others worry about; for I haven't the time to go through each detail. Many an official file could tell a story. Finally he ensconced himself in this city. Though without any of the usual accomplishments, he did have a keen glance and the airs of a philosopher.

Let's concede him the cleverness it took to contrive the nasty job of ousting me from the see. For that matter, I didn't actually hold it, nor did I have any position other than that of protecting and organizing the people. But he showed greater wisdom still. Like a true professional in the art of fraud, he didn't use outside help, he used myself to stage the whole business. I was a novice in these matters of course, and an entire stranger to intrigue for I had been trained to respect a different sort of cleverness—making a wise statement that is, or admiring the like from someone else, or extricating the inner meaning of Holy Scripture.

I should like to describe a novel feature of wicked behavior. It would be much simpler if everyone maintained a consistent character, either innocent of evil, or steeped in evil. People would do less injury to one another, because they would either side with one another or be openly at variance. But the good are the prey of the wicked, as it is. How very confused the human pattern is, and how very unfair God allows our associations to be. What man of reason can discern the miscreant as he plots, intrigues, contrives, continually uses every possible artifice to undermine him? The disposition with a slant towards evil is constantly watchful and keeps an eye on op-

805 portunity. Whereas the altruistic person is naturally slow and reluctant to suspect evil. And so honesty is easily trapped.

Consider for instance his subtlety in manipulating this matter. You will recognize another Egyptian Proteus.[48] He joins the group of the well-disposed, those altogether loyal to me.
810 Was there anyone who shared my roof, my table, my teaching, my plans as Maximus did? It was little wonder: he kept barking, like the great dog he was, against my enemies, and was an eager admirer of my sermons.
815 Simultaneously though, he was absorbing some of that disease that goes with pulpits, a remnant of the primal trouble.[49] I mean incessant jealousy, that ingrained fault; for wickedness is not easily reformed.
820 He chose two collaborators for the nasty business in hand, proving a good mentor in his own case, but an indifferent one in theirs. Both the one and the other were murderers; and when the offspring of the serpent was finally with difficulty disclosed one was found to be Belial fallen from his angelic
825 state. The other was a priest of this flock, more alien in his thinking than in appearance. He had never been overlooked or suffered any rebuff; but on the contrary he had always held first place in honor and dignity. Hear me, O Christ, the unerring eye of justice, if it be proper to invoke Christ in this in-
830 stance. Suddenly now he displayed his wicked and twisted hate.

CONSECRATION OF MAXIMUS, 831–999

Alas, how shall I lament the clear brilliance changed to darkness, the evil intrigue, the Egyptian cloud that burst upon me from afar? The first to come were the scouts, whom
835 the patriarch of the chosen land of Israel sent forth.[50] But the people who came were not wise men like Joshua and Caleb. Rather they were young and old in common guilt: Ammon,

---

48. For Proteus cf. Homer, *Od.* 4.365, 417–418.
49. Cf. Wis 2.24.   50. Cf. Nm 13.2.

Apammon, Harpocras, Stippas, Rhodon, Anubis, Hermanubis, the gods of Egypt, ape-shaped and doglike demons, miserable and corrupt sailors, venal creatures who would readily auction several gods, if there were several to auction.

Then a little later came those who sent the scouts. They were leaders worthy of such forces, or worthy kennelkeepers to give them a title more suitable for dogs. Like a bursting gourd filled with new wine or a brazen bellows loaded with air, I seethe inwardly with the many things I should like to say; but out of respect for the man who sent them, shallow though he be, I shall not say another word. Out of respect, too, for people who perhaps have some claim to forgiveness, because they were drawn astray through naiveté in whatever direction those miscreants, whom jealousy raised up against me here, led. You who are wise answer me this, since personally, unless the wise explain it to me, I cannot understand the performance. How was it that Peter himself, the leader of the bishops, originally installed me here with obviously unimpeachable titles, as his very correspondence with me shows, and honored me with the insignia of possession? But then suddenly a fawn was substituted for the maiden. This is by no means clear, and calls for explanation.

Of all the sorry jokes life plays, did one ever see anything more fit for the stage? A still more ludicrous detail remains. Some winebibber has made the statement that the most potent force of all is wine; someone else, a man truly wise, has said woman. Personally I should say gold holds the first place: it can easily call the tune for everything. Small wonder I suppose, seeing that we are more influenced by more material things than by the Spirit. But what would a Cynic have to do with money? Wait and see. A priest had come from Thasos bringing money from the church there for the purchase of Proconesian tiles.[51] Maximus got round him and made him an accomplice, suborning the wretched man by all sorts of promises. Villains readily consort with one another. He got

---

51. Proconesus is the modern Marmara, an island in the west part of the Propontis, noted for its marble quarries.

hold of the money—a trusty accomplice and a really efficient ally for any sort of huckstering. The proof lies in the fact that my closest associates, who respected me hitherto, now began to look on me as a sorry, penniless creature. Like a balance being tipped, they steadily leaned towards the other side.

At night, when I was indisposed, like thieving wolves in the fold they suddenly made their appearance, bringing a gang of hirelings from the fleet, the sort who make a typical Alexandrian mob. They burst in openly with the sailors, without any previous notice to the congregation, the church staff, or myself, who deserved at least a dog's treatment. They were all for consecrating the Cynic to the see, alleging that they had been commissioned to do this. For that's the kind of reward that Alexandria gives to service—I can only hope some other benevolent authority will requite you thus.

Dawn came. The clergy who lived close by grew agitated, and the news quickly went round from one to the other. A thorough commotion ensued, with a huge concourse of magistrates, strangers and riffraff. When people realized the sort of reward service was getting, everyone was beside himself because of the incident.

But I make the story overlong. Foiled in their purpose, they withdrew in resentment from my premises and, loth to relinquish their evil undertaking, acted out the wretched drama to the last. Repairing to the sordid dwelling of a flute-player, those reverent and beloved of God consecrated this villainous kennelkeeper before a congregation of miscreants. They didn't have to bind him as they tonsured, or use any pressure—our dog was quite ready for higher things. So the shears went at the well cultivated curls and the long labor of hands was effortlessly undone. The only misgiving caused by the operation was the disclosure of the mystery of the hair. All his strength lay in that, as was, they say, the case, once upon a time, of the judge Samson.[52] He was undone by having his hair shorn, an untimely and windblown harvest of tresses, gleaned by a woman to please his enemies.

52. Cf. Jgs 16.17.

So instead of a Cynic he was proclaimed a pastor, and again instead of a pastor a Cynic. What a shame! The poor shorn dog, deprived, on the one hand, of his beautiful hair, and, on the other, of a flock to administer, scuttling after bones in the marketplace once more! Whatever will you do about the glorious hair? Carefully cultivate it all again? Or go on being a laughing stock? A sorry dilemma indeed, and there's no real alternative except hanging. But tell us, where are you going to put the hair? Where will you send it? For exhibit in the theatre maybe? Or to the virgins? But which virgins? Your own Corinthian ladies? Those with whom, in religious intimacy you used to hold such exceedingly wise communication? Lucky dog, in heavenly company, say I.

Immediately, as a result of this outrageous performance, the city was so convulsed that everyone was furious. Bitter accusations flooded in about his manner of life, as indignation gave vent to what people were thinking. From every source different details were brought up by different people, all of which fitted in with his great *coup d'état*. Just like serious maladies in the human body, they have all sorts of minor ailments associated with them which lie dormant as long as the body is in health. In his case, too, the final performance served to publicize all his previous delinquencies. However, far be it from me to disclose them, they're known to the people who tell them. Personally, though I've been wronged by him, his previous record convulses me with shame.

"O come now, was he not, only yesterday, a friend of yours? Didn't you consider him worthy of the greatest praise?"[53] It's easy to run across people who know the details, and find fault with my naiveté at the time, in showing respect to the most inferior of Cynics. Indeed the ignorance I displayed deserves

---

53. Allusion to the eulogy (*Or.* 25, *In laudem Heronis philosophi*, PG 35. 1197–1225) Gregory had preached. Throughout the account, there is a clever sophistic play on the Cynic/dog association that is very difficult to reproduce in translation. J. Sajdak in *Eos* 15 (1909): 18–48, has a full discussion of the relations between the two men. Though not accepted by Theodosius, as late as Autumn, 381 A.D., Maximus was still recognized in the West. It seems also that subsequent to 381 he attacked Gregory in verse, cf., *Carmina de seipso*, XLI. *Adversus Maximum*, PG 37.1339.

censure. Like Adam I was undone by the nasty taste. To look at, the fruit that was really bitter seemed ripe. A style of conversation and protestations of loyalty that were skin deep only led me astray. For a trusting person is the easiest in the world to persuade since he is impulsively drawn to goodness, real or counterfeit. We are very conveniently constituted. To be sure each of us thinks what he wants to think.

But, all you wise folk, tell me what ought I have done? Which of you thinks he would have acted otherwise? The church was in such bad case in those days that one had to clutch at straws. When opportunities are limited, you have rather less power than when they abound. It was really a big thing for me to have a Cynic, instead of Herakles, following at my tail. And there was a bigger consideration still. His exile, actually for misdemeanors, he represented to me as laid upon him for God's sake; and though a rascal in reality, to me he was a conquering hero. If that is surprising, I must admit I've frequently made such mistakes. Surely, gentlemen, you will pardon me for erring on the generous side. He was in fact a reprobate, but I respected him as a decent man. I shall go further and lay down a stronger challenge. This talkative and tactless tongue I now stretch out resolutely for anyone who wishes to cut it off. But don't you think it actually is cut off? Very much so, you will agree, since it's been silent a long time. And it will be silent still longer maybe, to pay for its inopportune talk, and to learn that it shouldn't be benevolent to everyone. I shall add only one more consideration—see what you think of it. Wickedness is really impervious to reason. If decent treatment fails to sweeten a person, is there anything else under the sun that could do so? For in very truth my kindness to him constitutes his reproach. What attitude can one take to such a character, except repudiate him. If you believe this, don't probe any further. If you don't, then don't accept my former statements. But in fact nothing could be more incontrovertible.

SUBSEQUENT CAREER OF MAXIMUS, 1000–1043

And so the wretch made his miserable exit, or, to be more accurate, rather a good exit for the wretch he was. When the eastern Emperor during an offensive against barbarian tribes had his base in Thessalonica[54] our villainous dog started his intrigues again. Listen to the story. He got together that Egyptian rabble (the people who had shamelessly consecrated him) and betook himself to the camp, with the idea of securing the see for himself by imperial decree. He was thrown out like a dog, and then, in a great rage, with terrifying oaths (no one as yet was affected by the slander against me and opinion was sound) once more like a plague he fell upon Egypt. That was about the only right and wise move to make. He brought with him a hired gang of drifters and attached himself to Peter, whose pen was a double-edged weapon very apt to write a lot of conflicting things. He got the old man in a corner, and under threat of not letting him go demanded that the throne he sought be given to him. In the end the Prefect naturally became anxious about the fuss that was being created and, lest the trouble already caused should be aggravated, had him removed. At the moment he seems to be keeping quiet; but I'm afraid if this storm cloud brimming with hail is pushed by a strong wind, it will jettison its load upon the unsuspecting. Villainy of this kind is never really chastened; it may be held in check for the moment, but it's not going to learn wisdom.

There you have the "philosophy" of our modern Cynics. Barking dogs, true; but that's the extent of their Cynicism. Where's the resemblance to Diogenes, or Antisthenes? What has Crates to do with you people? Away, you say, with the entourage of Plato: the Stoa amounts to nothing. You, Socrates, held the foremost place up to now;[55] but I'm going to

---

54. On the base in Thessalonica see A. M. Ritter, *Das Konzil von Konstantinopel und Sein Symbol: Studien zur Geschichte und Theologie des II Oekumenische Konzils*, Forschungen zur Kirchen und Dogmengeschichte 15 (Göttingen 1965): 34.
55. "You, Socrates" cf. Diogenes Laertius, 2.37.

proclaim an oracle more infallible than that of the Delphic priestess: "Maximus is the wisest of all men." Surely I'm the most afflicted of all human beings. I have been since the beginning and am more so now. Such trials I've been delivered from, trials by land and perils by sea. But thank God for the fears: through them I have been wisely guided towards heavenly preoccupations, and I've succeeded in climbing beyond all impermanent things.

REACTION OF THE PEOPLE, 1045–1112

However, I felt thoroughly affronted on that occasion and, once I realized the villain had been consecrated, seized the opportunity with alacrity. Indeed, all my friends pressed upon me, actually keeping me under secret guard, watching over my comings and goings and all my movements. All my enemies, on the other hand, when they witnessed the conflict, were of the opinion that the schism would bring the dissolution of orthodoxy. I realized all this and made up my mind not to put up with it. My plight was that of a man whose simplicity (I shan't deny it) is greater than his wisdom. Straightway I backed water, as the saying goes, but not very skilfully. I shouldn't have attracted notice. But as it was, a sort of valedictory remark escaped my lips, wrung from the depths of fatherly affection. "The Trinity, which in paternal generosity I gave to my yearning children, may you preserve unimpaired; and, my dearest friends, be mindful of my labors."

When the congregation heard this, one of the more irrepressible cried out. Then immediately, like a swarm of bees driven by smoke, they sprang up and burst into uncontrolled shouting. Men, women, girls and boys, children, old people, nobles, common folk, magistrates, soldiers on furlough: they all seethed equally with indignation against my enemies in yearning for their pastor. However I was not one to bend the knee to pressure, or to accept authority unless lawfully bestowed. I could not even be forced to accept it when it was lawful.

They tried another means of getting their way. With many oaths and entreaties they besought me at least to come and succour them, not to abandon my flock to wolves. How could I avoid weeping? O Anastasia,[56] most glorious of churches, you kindled again the faith that had lain prostrate. Ark of Noah,[57] you alone escaped the flooding of the universe and the seeds you bore contained a second universe of orthodoxy. From every quarter people came crowding in to you, regarding this as a tremendous crisis. Was I going to win, or would the congregation have its way?

There I stood before them, speechless, beset by darkness. I was unable either to repress their shouting or promise anything they asked, being helpless in the first instance, fearful in the second. The heat began to be oppressive and perspiration rolled. Women, especially the mothers among them, lost their voices in the panic, and children were crying. The day was waning. They all swore they would not give up their efforts, even if it meant dying in their tracks in the actual church, without having some concession to their wishes, the sort of concession that is wrung from one by sheer weariness. Alas for the sense of hearing. Why wasn't I struck deaf there and then?

"Tell us then, are you going to have the Trinity thrown out with yourself?" Finally, panic-stricken lest something awful happen, I gave my word, and they accepted that on the strength of my character. I swore no oath however—I am not a swearing man, if I, too, may boast a little in God, by whom I have been cleansed in the grace of the Spirit. I said I would stay on until some of the bishops arrived (they were expected at the time), thinking that then I could extricate myself from these uncongenial anxieties. And so with some difficulty we dispersed, each side victorious because of a spark of hope.

---

56. On Anastasia see *Or.* 42. 26, *Supremum vale*, PG 36.489–492, NPNF, ser. 2, 7.294.
57. On the church as Ark of Noah cf. J. Daniélou, *Primitive Christian Symbols* (Baltimore 1963), 58–70.

They thought they had succeeded in retaining me, and I thought my stay would be quite brief.

SUBSEQUENT PREACHING AND CONTROVERSY, 1113–1272

That was the situation. Once again orthodox teaching cast its light, being very quickly reinforced, as when swift generalship and rallying throngs buttressed a rampart or a defense line where it has weakened. People who previously had been attached to my doctrine, and sided with me only because of that, began to approve of me more when they saw how I had been treated.

One group was drawn by the actual preaching of the Trinity. For a considerable time indeed the doctrine had been absent from preaching. As if (I hesitate to say it) it had been long buried, this tenet that was at once native and from an outside source. It was there once: then it waned: then it came back again, demonstrating the resurrection from the tomb.

With another group my personal preaching perhaps had some weight. There were those who rushed to me as they would to a strong athlete, and those who were glad to hold on to me as a creation of their own. As for you, let some of you enquire about these matters from those who know them well, and others tell the tale to those who don't know—if there be any such people who live so far away from you, or who are, even now, outside of the Roman empire. And so the tale can be told to future generations too, as another instance of the fresh troubles in life liable to be brought by the vain march of time. More evil is woven into the pattern than good.

I have not so far mentioned the congregation which stood fast in orthodoxy, that noble offspring born out of my birth pangs. Of them it can be said that when no orthodox teacher was available, they betook themselves to any teacher that was, like people parched to whatever moisture they could find, or people beset by darkness making for a tiny light. Doctrine was for them the succour of their famine. What is one to say about these strangers to the faith, when one remembers how they delighted in doctrine?

A CATALOG OF HERESIES, 1146–1186

The paths which lead from the straight and ordered road are exceedingly numerous, and they all lead to the pit of destruction into which the evil one has plunged the image. In order to provide himself with a loophole from that place, he divides opinions, not tongues, as God himself did once.[58]

From that place spring the aberrations in doctrine. There are people who have no knowledge of God beyond the force that brings everything into being and sustains it; people who posit a multitude of gods instead of one and worship figments of their own; people who will not admit of any providence where this world is concerned, and analyze everything according to the movement of the stars. And then there are those who were the chosen people of God, but crucified the Son to honor the Father: And people whose piety is a matter of trivial precepts, who deny angels, spirits, the resurrection, the writings of the prophets: And people who worship Christ in the shadows of the Law, and the followers of Simon Magus, who revere Abyss and Silence and the bisexual Aeons as natures that preceded time.

Sprung from them are those who concoct deity out of scripture, who allot the Old and New Testaments to two separate gods, an austere and a beneficent; who posit three static natures, Spirit, Earth, and the element in between. There are those who delight in the primal darkness of Mani, and those who pay unholy cult to the spirit of Montanus, or the hollow pride of Novatian. And there are the destroyers, too, of the incorruptible Trinity, the dividers of the indivisible nature. Again from these latter as from a single hydra, spring many heads of impiety: the teaching that puts among created things the Holy Spirit only; that which classifies the Son, too, with

58. Cf. Gn 11.1–9.

the Spirit; those who introduce a god who is coeval with Caesar; those who bring in the outrageous notion of Docetism; those who say the Son on earth was a second son; those who maintain that what was saved was not perfect and was without *nous*.

GREGORY'S METHODS, 1187–1272

All those are splinters, if I may use a figure, from the tree of orthodoxy, and they have given origin to monstrous errors. But in those days was there any one of these people so steadfast as not to bend an ear to my teaching? Some were influenced by the force of what I had to say: others became tractable because of the way in which I said it. For I chose my language very carefully, avoiding controversy or ridicule. I spoke in sorrow, did not lash out, did not (like some people) capitalize on easy and smooth opportunities. For power and persuasion have nothing in common. Nor did I try to conceal bad reasoning with bluff—this is a very tricky performance, squirting up ink from the depths like a cuttlefish and routing my critics by a smoke screen. On the contrary, I was gentle and suave in my preaching, regarding myself as the proponent of a doctrine that is sympathetic and mild, and smites no one. For yielding is reasonable, and winning is much more admirable when someone is drawn to God by the force of persuasion. Such are the principles engraved on *my* tablets.

Another principle of my training, well and wisely engraved, is this: not to make the mistake of regarding a facile and dubious eloquence as the only road of piety: Not to be hail-fellow-well-met in theaters, in the square, at parties, amid laughter and singing,[59] before my own tongue was purged of unseemly language. Not to pour the mysteries of doctrine wantonly into profane ears alien to Christ, making fun of things which are studied only with effort. On the contrary, I should fulfil the commandments as perfectly as possible by

---

59. Cf. *Or.* 27.2, *Adversus Eunomianos*, SC 250.72.

ministering to the poor,⁶⁰ exercising hospitality, tending the sick, persevering in psalmody, prayer, groaning, tears, prostration on the ground, restraints upon the belly, mortifications of the senses, of impulse, of laughter, control of the tongue, lulling the flesh by the power of the spirit.

There are actually many ways of salvation, all leading to fellowship with God.⁶¹ These ways one must tread, not that way only which depends on eloquence. The language of even a simple faith suffices, and indeed it is by such faith that God, for the most part, leads effortlessly to salvation. If faith were the province of the wise alone nothing in our world would be poorer than God. If you are full of anxiety and desirous of eloquence, and put out if you do not produce a copious flow (even in this instance my prayer for you is human), speak, but speak with fear, not always, not everything, nor before everybody, nor everywhere.⁶² There are proper audiences, proper measures, proper places and proper times. Everything has its opportune moment,⁶³ as you know; and the mean is best, as one of the sages said.⁶⁴ The territories of the Mysians and the Phrygians are far apart: so too are my brand of eloquence and that of seculars. Their speeches are made for display before gatherings of young men on fictitious topics, where results, or lack of results, don't matter much. There's nothing more insubstantial than shadow. But in my case, where the aim is to speak the truth, it's a matter of grave concern how the speech turns out. The way is beset by pitfalls, to tumble off is obviously to fall to the gates of hell.

Consequently one must be exceedingly careful to use language wisely on the one hand, and to listen to it wisely on the other. And there are times when both one and the other are

---

60. On Gregory's ministry to poor cf. *Or.* 14, *De pauperum amore*, PG 35.857–909.
61. See Gregory's *Comparatio Vitarum*, H. M. Werhahn, ed., *Gregorii Nazianzeni*, 69 n.156.
62. He discusses the theologian and his audience at greater length in *Or.* 28, *De theologia*, SC 250.100ff.
63. Eccl 3.1.
64. Cf. Stobaeus, 3 1.172a 1, also quoted in *Or.* 43, *Funebris oratio in laudem Basilii Magni Caesareae in Cappadocia episcopi*, PG 36.573.

to be avoided: the prudent yardstick of fear should be used. Listening of course is less dangerous than speaking, and less dangerous still is absenting oneself altogether. There's no point in deadening one's mind by taking a drug[65] or in approaching the breath of a mad dog.[66] So I learned from the oracles of scripture in which, before my mind was formed, I was brought up.

And so as a pastor of citizens and visitors I was by that time a prosperous husbandman, even though my harvest was not completely assembled. I had but recently gleaned some of them from the thorns; the ground was being smoothed for others; in others still, the seed was being sown.[67] Some were not weaned, the growth of some was over ground, some were turning green, some bearing ears of corn, some ripening, some white for the harvest. The threshing floor held some, and some the grateful barn. Some were being winnowed, and some were among the grain. Some had reached the goal of husbandry and were already bread, a bread that would not now nourish the weary husbandman indeed, but people who had lost no sweat.

ADVENT OF THEODOSIUS, 1273-1324

My wish would have been to bring my narrative to a close at this point, and to say nothing of matters that are unworthy of record. However at this juncture the march of events makes that impossible. Some of the subsequent developments were good: of others I don't know what I ought to say, to what fate to attribute them, or which to approve. While I was in this case, suddenly the Emperor[68] arrived from Macedonia. He had put a halt to the barbarian turbulence: they were overkeen as a result of their own numbers and daring. In the

65. Plato, *Meno*, 80a.
66. Galen, *De locis affectis libri vi*, C. G. Kühn, ed., *Claudi Galeni opera omnia* (Leipzig 1821, reprint Hildesheim 1964):8.423.
67. Mk 4.26.
68. On Theodosius, vv.1282-1289, see A. M. Ritter, *Das Konzil*, 225.

matter of shepherding simpler natures towards the faith of God he was not a bad man, and he was wondrously devoted to the Trinity. For this doctrine must be thoroughly ingrained in all those who presume to occupy securely a stable throne. Nevertheless his zeal of spirit was not the kind to emulate previous performances by present action using the opportunity of the moment, that is, to undo the mistakes of the past. Or, while he may have had zeal enough, he had not the boldness necessary, nor the daring. How shall I say it—give me the word? Perhaps, instead, I should say vision.

I do not consider it good practice to coerce people instead of persuading them. Persuasion has more weight with me, and indeed with those very people I direct towards God. Whatever is done against one's will, under the threat of force, is like an arrow artificially tied back, or a river dammed in on every side of its channel. Given the opportunity it rejects the restraining force. What is done willingly, on the other hand, is steadfast for all time. It is made fast by the unbreakable bonds of love.

The Emperor, it seems to me, keeps this in mind, and to this extent keeps fear within bounds, winning over everybody gently and setting up voluntary action as the unwritten law of persuasion. I need not say what a gracious ruler he is to his more than grateful subjects, what respect he has shown me from our first meeting, what kind things he said and how kindly he listened. It would be a great shame for me if, being what I am, I should give the impression of concern with sentiment of this kind. One thing alone claims my respect, and that is God.

"God" he said, "through me hands the church over to you and to your labors." This was scarcely credible until it actually happened; because, with tension widespread and at a high pitch, the city population was fully determined not to give way but to hold on to what they had even at the cost of unpleasant incidents. Coercing them would mean that their exacerbation would be vented on myself, who am so easily intimidated. However that was what he said, and I was suffused by a glow of pleasure not unmixed with apprehension. O Christ, who by thy suffering dost summon us to suffer, in that hour Thou wert the arbiter of my struggles. So now become my helper in my woes.

TRIUMPHAL PROCESSION, 1325–1395

1325 But to go on with the story. Armed forces, drawn up in the various aisles, invested the church. An agitated mob confronted them, like the sand of the sea, or snow, or storm-tossed waves. Their mood veered between hostility and entreaty; hostility towards me but entreaty where the civil power was concerned. Every place was crowded, the streets, the arenas, the piazzas. Men and women, children and old folk, craned down from second and third stories. Struggles, groans, tears and grumblings gave the impression of a town being sacked by force.

And the noble leader was myself, sickly and decrepit, the breath scarcely left in my carcass, marching between general and army, my eyes raised to heaven. Hope sustained me as we wound our way, until finally I stood in the church, I know not how. And here's an item worth recounting. Of the events of that day, many thought it more eloquent than a sermon. They take the view that, at very crucial moments particularly, nothing that one sees is without significance. For my part, though I'm more averse to miracles than most, I cannot disbelieve what they say. Withholding credence indiscriminately is worse than overcredulity: you have shallowness in one case, assumption in the other.

But what was the marvel? Let my book proclaim it to the world, lest such a great grace escape the notice of posterity. It was daybreak; but because the orb of the sun was obscured by a cloud, night overlay the whole city. This was a highly unpropitious circumstance for the occasion, since a festivity more than anything else demands serene conditions. My enemies, as if God were showing His displeasure with the preformance, were gleeful and I was masking in my own mind my depression.

Then when the purple-robed Emperor and myself were inside the chancel gate of the sanctuary, at the invocation, the mingled praise of God by everyone was borne aloft with cheering and outstretched hands. Thereupon, at the command of God, the cloud was dispersed and sunlight blazed out brilliantly, with the result that the whole edifice, previously in gloom, was immediately lit up as if by lightning. Everyone was struck by the appearance of the old tabernacle bathed in heavenly radiance. Countenances and spirits brightened everywhere.

At that stage, in a surge of popular enthusiasm to keep pace with the spectacle, people began to cry out with all their strength demanding me, as if the moment lacked only myself for completion. A first and greatest favor preferable to thrones, they said, could be bestowed by imperial power on the city, if I were placed on the episcopal throne. The request came from people in power as well as the common people, all clamoring with equal intensity. It came from women—they raised their voices higher indeed than is altogether decorous for the sex. The reverberating thunder was unbelievable. Finally I made one of my retinue rise from his seat, I myself had no voice left, so tense was I and so exhausted by fear. By means of that other I made the following pronouncement.

"Silence, you people, cease the shouting. This is above all an occasion for thanksgiving. Later on will be a suitable time for greater issues." To this there was a murmur of assent from the congregation, for moderation appeals to everyone. The Emperor himself commended me and took his departure. Such was the issue of this assembly, which had terrified me to the extent only that a single sword, drawn and sheathed to control the turbulence of an excited populace, can cause apprehension.

CONDUCT AS PATRIARCH, 1396–1505

How to continue the narrative of subsequent events, which as events go had some importance, leaves me puzzled. Would some chronicler volunteer to finish the story? Even though others should extol me, I feel embarrassed by having my praises sung. It goes against my principles. I shall continue however, with as much modesty as I can summon.

I kept indoors. Now that the church had been taken over, the city had ceased its tumult. There were, however, subdued rumblings, as in the case of the giant who, according to the story, was struck by a thunderbolt near the mount of Aetna. He kept on belching smoke and fire from the depths.

In the name of God, what *was* the right course of action for me? Tell me, you group of callow youngsters who are now in power. You think of gentleness as weakness and consider that courage must be savage and frenetic. The question was whether by a flagrant use of power and opportunity to push, drive, plunder and devastate; or to heal with the medicine of salvation.[69] The latter course had two notable advantages: people could be made moderate by the use of moderation, and I was in a position to win glory and affection for myself. It was the right procedure naturally, the one I propose always and openly to follow. I followed it then when I had my best opening.

I want to make it clear, in the first place, that I was not attributing more to the favorable turn of events than to the power of God. Why should I, who had as my soundest adviser common sense, seek counsel from an august source? Everyone courts the majesty of those in power, particularly those with a confidential position, people who are devoid of manhood except where money is concerned. Is there any point in describing the style and artifices of those who cleave to the very doors of the palace, laying accusations, pilfering outrageously, making a wretched traffic out of religion, being generally shameless, to put it in a nutshell? I was alone in choosing to be loved rather than hated. I won respect by keeping to myself, and devoting myself for the most part to God and the pursuit of perfection. The doors of the mighty I left to others.

69. Cf. *Or.* 31.25, *De spiritu sancto*, SC 250.324.

Furthermore, when I perceived that some people were embarrassed by the realization that they had wronged me, while the others were very naturally in turn seeking favors from me, I allayed the fears of the first group and did actually help the latter.

So far as my resources went, I treated everyone according to his particular need. To give an example I shall relate just one incident. Once I was confined indoors by illness. It certainly was the invariable companion of my troubles, though hostile people, of course, will take the view that I was malingering.[70] While I was thus laid up, suddenly some people made their way inside, bringing with them a young man, pallid, long-haired, poorly dressed. I made the feeble sort of attempt to get up that a panic-stricken person will. The people, however, simply voiced their customary thanks to God and to the emperor for making this day possible. They added some words of praise for myself and then took their leave. Thereupon the young man, speechless and terrified, threw himself at my feet as suppliant. I kept asking him who he was, where he came from, what he wanted; but the only reply I got was louder cries. He swore, he moaned, he tightened his grip on my hands. I began to find myself very close to tears.

When words were of no avail he was dragged away forcibly. Then one of those standing by remarked: "This man is your would-be assassin, for it is by the grace of God you are alive. He is here of his own free will, to pass sentence on his own guilt, a kindly murderer, a noble accuser, who offers his tears as penalty for blood."

I was utterly broken by these words, and hastened to say something that would obliterate all unpleasantness. "God save you. For me, who have been delivered, to be kind to my attacker is but a little thing. Your courage has made you mine. See to it that you become a credit both to me and to God." The city, for you can't keep good hidden, was immediately mollified by my reaction, just like iron by the action of fire.[71]

70. On this bizarre incident with a would-be assassin cf. P. Gallay, *La vie*, 190.
71. Cf. Plato, *Rep.* 411a.

But what do you think of this? I accepted the fact that I could not find the slightest written record among the papers of my predecessors in the see of the notorious sums of money, the treasures and revenues from every quarter, which had been piling up from subscriptions by the greatest churches of the world: Nor in the files of the treasurers who are in charge of such matters. That I accepted, and I did not, as some people kept recommending and urging me to do, bring in any outside person at all to make an audit that would discredit religion.

A man is responsible only for what he has, not for what he claims by right of inheritance. People who care about money will doubtless criticize this, but it will be readily accepted by those who are above money. Greed is a bad passion which besets everyone, but in the domain of the spirit it has an added wickedness. If everyone had this attitude towards money we should never find such an amount of it in churches, a thing which is not to my liking. I am speaking of clerics, of course, who should be near God.

It was the gossip of my opponents, too, that the congregation would not reach even to the doors. During the bad period for me, I was so thoroughly disparaged by everyone that the congregation had been divided. But now the churches with their full complement were in my hands.

I made all this my earnest concern, not to mention the work of administering the poor, the young virgins, strangers, guests, prisoners, psalmody, night-long tears, men and women practising continence, and all the other matters that it pleases God to see in good order.

COUNCIL OF CONSTANTINOPLE, 1506–1571[72]

Destructive envy however was not idle. Either openly or secretly everything falls under its domain. It was my power

72. On the Council of Constantinople see D. J. Constantelos, "Toward the Convocation of the Second Ecumenical Synod," *Greek Orthodox Theological Re-*

actually which proved the source of disaster. All the bishops of the East, except for Egypt, from the most remote corners of land and sea, right up as far as the second Rome, stirred by counsels of the Lord that I cannot guess at, convened in council. Their object was to consolidate orthodox doctrine.

Presiding over them was a man saintly, simple, straightforward, redolent of God, serene of countenance, impressing those who saw him with his blend of courage and modesty, a true product of the Spirit. Can there be any doubt about the man I mean, the bishop of the church of Antioch? He was what he was named and he was named what he was, Meletius (honeyed) in nature and in name. For the sake of the Holy Spirit he had endured much (even if he had been somewhat deceived at the hands of a stranger), and in these splendid struggles he was fervent in grace. On the august throne, then, the bishops installed me. I cried out and groaned, but, for one particular reason, was not altogether unwilling. The reason? Bear witness to it, O Logos, for it is not right to hide the truth.

A wish readily begets hope, and everything seems easy when one's spirit is high: personally I am perhaps inclined to be oversanguine in such matters. I thought, in my vain imaginings, that once I had control of this throne (outward show carries great weight) I could act like a chorus leader between two choruses. Putting the two groups chorus-fashion, one on this side of me, the other on that, I could blend them with myself and thus weld into a unity what had been so badly divided.

The division certainly ran deep. It was a matter for copious tears, copious lament and agony. Never among the disasters of ancient or recent time had there been the like. So much woe had befallen so many that it surpassed even the notorious

---

view 27 (1982): 395–405, G. H. Ettlinger, "The Holy Spirit in the Theology of the Second Ecumenical Synod and the Undivided Church," Ibid., 431–440, D. J. Geanakopolos, "The Second Ecumenical Synod of Constantinople (381): Proceedings and Theology of the Holy Spirit," Ibid., 407–429, V. Peri, "Risonanze storiche e contemporanee del secondo concilio ecumenico," *Ann.Hist.Conc.* 14 (1982): 13–57, A. M. Ritter, *Das Konzil,* J. Vogt, "Konzilsjubilaen im Jahre 1981," *Ann.Hist.Conc.* 14 (1982): 257–270.

division of Israel launched by Christ-slaying hatred. The leaders and teachers of the people, donors of the Spirit, whose doctrine of salvation is poured forth from high thrones, who constantly with booming voices preach peace to everyone publicly in churches, raged bitterly against one another. And as they clamored, gathered support, accused and were accused, jumped from their seats beside themselves, appropriated to their side anyone they could get to first in a furious struggle for power and control (I have no words really to stigmatize such goings on), they burst the whole universe apart. It was exactly as I said when I began the narrative.

The difference in mentality between east and west appeared more profound than that of geography and climate. On these latter scores there is common ground in the middle regions if not at the extremes; but on the former there is no link at all to bind the dissidents. Concern about religion was not the real cause (this was an invention of chagrin, which is an accomplished liar), but rivalry about thrones. Why do I say this about bishops? I do not mean the bishops so much (for I know both parties fairly well) as those partisans on either side, winds that fanned the flame that has been kindled, and very cleverly looked to their friends to advance their own interests. Did I say cleverly? I mean, of course, contemptibly.

MELETIUS DIES, GREGORY'S PROPOSAL, 1572–1678

However, even I gained something from the confusion. The bishop of Antioch whom I just mentioned, full of measured and unmeasured years, made many conciliatory recommendations, I hear, that he was formerly known to air among his friends. But then he departed from this world to join the choir of angels. Amid elaborate ceremony, and a concourse of the city folk, who were affected, it is said, in unprecedented fashion, his remains were despatched to his own diocese, there to be a treasured possession for those who knew him. A proposal then came before us that did not merit consideration; but it had the vociferous support of the turbulent and wicked element. They were anxious to set up another bishop against the man[73] who was now the sole occupant of the throne. Both sides made many recommendations, either conciliatory or liable to provoke trouble. At that stage I myself made the suggestions I thought best, and likely to solve difficulties.[74]

"My friends, you don't all seem to me to grasp the situation, nor do I get the impression that you regard the matter before us as worth discussion. You seem to be missing the proper path by the widest margin. You are concerned with a single city only, and want to make that a center of even greater strife at this stage. With that sort of object in view you seek a helping hand from me. But I am concerned with greater and fuller issues. Consider this great orb of the earth, which has been sealed with the flowing blood of the Savior, for which God suffered in the form of a man, giving himself as a ransom to deliver us. And there have been many other lesser victims too. Let us suppose that two angels are struggling for the city. Now not even these (and my remark is wrung from pain) are worth such great concern. On the contrary, by the very fact that they are angels, they ought to be far above strife and nastiness, since what is superior should have superior treatment.

"While the saintly bishop was with us, and while it was yet unclear how those of the west, in their former exacerbated mood, would receive him, it was to some degree understandable that those who call themselves defenders of the law should be somewhat aggrieved. For a gentle man is a cure for anger, and presumption is much strengthened by ignorance. Now, however, what do I suggest? There is no upheaval now, God has brought calm to His affairs. Please accept my recommendation—it displays foresight and more wisdom than the suggestions of the young. We old men cannot hope to convince the excited element, of course, who are always subject to vainglory. Let the throne pass into the possession of

---

73. *i.e.*, Paulinus.
74. On Gregory's "Friedensrede" (vv.1591–1679) see A. M. Ritter, *Das Konzil*, 254.

the man who has held it up to now. It will be perfectly natural if according to ancient custom we mourn the deceased a little longer. Then old age itself, the inevitable and noble consummation common to human kind, will provide a solution for the problem. When this man comes to die, and goes where for long he has yearned to go, rendering his spirit to the God who gave it to him, then, with the harmonious consent of all the people and of the wise bishops, we shall under the guidance of the Holy Spirit appoint another to the throne.

"The only possible solution to our difficulties would be achieved in this way. The point is: we shall either gain the greater end and bring over the estranged element (at the moment the west, I perceive, is estranged), or we shall gain the limited objective of restoring harmony to the city, a population of such importance that has been exhausted by the long duration of the trouble. Let's have an end at long last to this worldwide upheaval: let's have compassion on those who are now in schism, on those who are very nearly in that state, and on the generations yet to come. No one ought to concern himself with conjectures about what the issue will be, if this point of view prevails through mere passage of time. We are actually at the point of crisis now. We have the choice of continuing to preserve our noble and revered doctrine, or of seeing it disappear as a result of dissension.

"For just as a fault in the paint is laid at the door (albeit wrongly) of the painter, so the character of disciples is debited to the masters. If the mystic turns out bad, how much greater is the sin against the mystery of the mystagogue? We should yield a little so that we may win a greater victory, our own salvation under God, and the salvation of the world which has been so pitiably devastated. Victory is not a matter of glory from every angle. It is better to cede something with profit than to hold on to it with blame. This is known to the Trinity, and it is the lesson of my successful preaching carried through boldly in the face of stonings.

"I have simply and justly put forward this day the suggestions I know will further our objectives. Certainly there are people among us burdened with gold, and equally with greed, who traffic in sacred offices. Thus, if there be anyone, himself doubtless a bought man, who is base enough to think that my suggestion is designed to curry favor, or that I am scheming for some private end as many people do and trying to conceal my own intrigues, or that I am motivated by the desire for power myself, let the judgment be left to the final fire. What I request from you is a throneless life. It may be without prestige, but it is without danger. I shall go and take up my abode where one is completely free from the wicked. That is better than being involved with people, being unable to bring others to one's view, or on the other hand to side with views that conflict with reason. Let the man who knows the throne come forward here. He will find he has to deal with many people both worthy and unworthy. I offer this for your consideration. It is my final word."

REACTION TO HIS SPEECH, 1680–1689

My speech was the signal for screams on every side from that flock of crows all massed together. The horde of young men, a new-fangled party, gave the impression of dust churned up by a whirlwind during a storm. In their confused chattering not even a ruler backed by reverential fear and authority could have managed to reason with them. They were like a swarm of wasps suddenly darting up in one's face and, far from attempting to chasten them, the august assembly of the elders actually joined the demonstration.

THE EASTERN PREROGATIVE, 1690–1704

Reflect on the excellence of their reasoning. Matters, they argued, should be accommodated to the east-west motion of the sun. Everything had begun where God shone upon us in the semblance of the flesh.[75] Good heavens! Let us learn not

---

75. The fact that Christ became incarnate in Palestine was apparently used as argument for Eastern superiority. See A. M. Ritter, *Das Konzil*, 254.

to make the seasons objects of reverence, but to regard the flesh of Christ as the first fruits of the whole human race. One could very well retort that if He began in the place where boldness held greater sway, it was so that He might the more easily be put to death there, and from that the resurrection follow, and from that salvation. Surely people who put forward such views should have yielded to those who, as I said, showed a mature understanding. It demonstrated the extent generally of their conceit.

ANARCHY IN THE COUNCIL, 1705–1744

Then there was this. The sweet and limpid sources of ancient faith, which sprang long ago from the deliberations of Nicaea, which unified the sacred nature of the Trinity, I saw being miserably befouled by the brackish inflow of ideas from either side. Those who shaped the powers that be could congratulate themselves on being styled moderates. Open supporters of the extremists might be nearer the truth. They were bishops who were just then in the process of learning about God. Teachers yesterday, pupils again today, initiators into mysteries where they themselves have to become initiators after the event, they infect congregations with their own bad doctrines. And yet, I can't understand how, they insist on having the floor—with never a tear, mind you. Just imagine, a full recital of one's diseases without so much as a tear.

So much for that particular performance. People say that everyone is the slave of the moment. In any case it's very pleasant to have some fun. Generally speaking humor can't be achieved by effort, or by any other shift either—you can't even buy it. Overkindly as I tend to be, however did I manage it? In front of the pulpit I made a proclamation, shouting out to everyone. "Come along here then, anyone that likes. You may be two-sided, many-sided, it doesn't matter. The party (it's an open house!) is on. If the dice throw goes against you (and nothing changes face so easily as opportunity), you know the technique. Change sides again. It's not really smart to stay with one conviction. It pays to be very versatile in life."

What came of that?⁷⁶ The multiform dream image that was of old, gold first, then silver, bronze, iron, and the feet of shell. Stone, I'm afraid, whittles it all away. Of old there was no entry to the church for Moabites and Ammonites: now there is. "But tell us, didn't you formerly approve all this? Who was in charge of the assemblies? What were the assemblies like, who made them up?" I hate having to say it once more, because it shames me. They were at the beck of everybody, which is to say of nobody. Where you have too many in charge you have anarchy.

GREGORY LEAVES THE ASSEMBLY, 1745–1795

Fortunately illness came to my rescue, because it kept me for the most part at home. I had only one idea in mind, to get away. There lay the total solution to my problems. Whatever decision was reached, let it have the force of law. There were some people who retained enough independence to go on meeting. They did so under constraint and with difficulty, but they did meet. They were deceived by the ambiguous nature of the doctrines set forth and by the ostensibly orthodox character of the preaching; but they were screened by their own ignorance of evil. They were in fact a breed totally different from their predecessors. Personally, the day that someone can blend the fragrance of unalloyed myrrh with filth, I shall be prepared to accept this large mob of traffickers in Christ. It's so much easier to get involved with evil than with good.

This group disapproved of fresh opinion (which is a name the headstrong have for foresight); but then foresight made one equally disapproving of them. It was like Lot and the patriarch Abraham.⁷⁷ One took one road, the other the opposite lest they should be embarrassed by the sight of their possessions. It seems unnecessary to recount the variety and

76. Cf. Dn 2.31ff.   77. Cf. Gn 13.8ff.

nature of the arguments whereby those closest to me tried to influence these grey hairs. While making initial concessions they demanded from the trustworthy Gregory (alas!) a solid undertaking. They were trustworthy themselves, but trustworthy intriguers. The undertaking was that I should cooperate in everything. Imagine, in everything! Who conceived the egregious notion that I could be led to anything by sheer numbers rather than by God the Word? Water shall flow upwards or fire take the opposite course before I yield up one whit of my salvation.

After that I withdrew into privacy. The move was obvious in that I actually changed my place of abode, dragging myself from the recesses of the church far from evil assemblies and arguments. What laments they made though, those that kept pressure on me! Omitting mention of the measures taken by others, the congregation above all cried out in supplication. They raised their hands to heaven, swore oaths, mourned me as if I were already dead. When I recall the misery and the tears! How steel one's feelings to endure it? "We hear you are going to abandon us, your own flock, meagre once upon a time, but now an abundant harvest. The people you have converted: some of them standing outside your doors which it only remains for you to open; some already inside; some others in search of those outside. To whom will you relinquish them? Who will nourish your brood? Have respect for these very labors that have worn you down. Give what remains of your life to us and to God. Let our church be the one to dispatch you on your final journey."

RESIGNATION, 1796–1871

All this was a severe pressure, but I held out. Presently God gave me a way of escape.[78] The Egyptian and Macedonian contingents arrived. They had been hurriedly summoned in the hope of providing some peaceful settlement, for they are

---

78. On vv.1797ff. see A. M. Ritter, *Das Konzil*, 97–111.

the framers of the laws and mysteries of God. It was as if a harsh western wind blew in upon us. The delegates of the eastern provinces opposed them resolutely. If I may imitate tragic language somewhat, they sharpened their fierce tusks like boars, looked cross-eyed with fiery glance, and joined battle. Many discussions took place which generated more heat than light, and they fixed upon some pettifogging detail which concerned myself, by turning up regulations that were long obsolete,[79] an issue on which I was in fact obviously and fully exonerated.

There was no question of hostility to myself, nor any anxiety to secure the throne for others. By no means. The measure was directed against those who had enthroned me, a fact that was made fully clear to me in confidential exchange. They could not, they felt, countenance the insult to themselves, which concerned older issues as well as recent happenings. All the time, like a tethered horse,[80] though worn out by troubles and sickness, I continued to plunge in my stable. I neighed pitiably, vexed by my bonds, and longed for pastures and freedom. When they raised the issue I mentioned, I joyfully seized upon the pretext and broke free from my bonds. Clearly I could never convince power seekers of this, but it is the truth. The opportunity was there. I came forward and spoke as follows:

"Gentlemen, God has brought you together so that you may determine something that He would wish. As for my own affairs, let them take second place; since, in the business of such an important assembly, it is really trivial what the outcome be, even though my elevation has been in vain. You should raise your minds to a higher consideration. Be reconciled, unite, however belatedly. How long must we go on being a laughingstock? People regard us as insensitive creatures devoid of any feeling except combat. Please join hands with a good will in a gesture of fellowship. Now I become Jonas the prophet. I am giving myself as victim for the safety of the ship, even

79. Canon 15 of the Council of Nicaea, see A. M. Ritter, ibid.
80. Cf. Homer, *Il.* 6.506, Vergil, *Aen.* 11.492.

though it will be a case of the innocent encountering the waves. Take me then on the issue of the lot and cast me forth, the hospitable whale will welcome me from the depths. From now on begin to be of one mind, and then make your way towards everything in due order. Let this place be known as the place of spaciousness,[81] and then I shall have played a not ignoble part. If you persist with me, I shall have this single criticism—that you are making a conflict over thrones. If you take the view that I suggest, nothing will be difficult. When I was enthroned it was without enthusiasm, and now I take my leave with a will. My state of health, too, suggests this course. I have only one death to die and that is in the hands of God. But, O my Trinity, you are all I care for. What tongue will you have, trained for your defense? An independent one, I hope, and full of zeal. Fare you well, gentlemen, and be mindful of my labors."

They were taken aback at my remarks. I took my leave in a mood alternating between joy and some depression, joy because I was getting some respite from trouble, pain because I knew not what would become of the people. It is always an agony to be deprived of one's children, and it was in my case. God knows and they know if more lay beneath the surface than appeared, shipwreck and reefs, the snares of the deep. Others talk of that. I shall hold my peace, I have no time to unravel base intrigues. I practice simplicity of heart, the source of salvation, which is my sole concern. This much I do know. Straightway I was accorded the honor of a more enthusiastic assent than is altogether polite. Such are the favors reserved by our fatherland for the deserving. So much for that.

INTERVIEW WITH THEODOSIUS, 1872–1918

But what about the emperor? Did I fawn, or prostrate myself, or clasp his right hand, or make any suppliant speech? Did I try to bring forward ambassadors from among my

---

81. Cf. Gn 26.33.

friends, particularly the better disposed to me among the magistrates? In my anxiety to avoid losing so great a throne did I lavish gold, that mighty conqueror? Such shifts I leave to other very adroit persons. Precisely as I was, I made haste to the palace, and there were several present who witnessed what ensued.

"All-powerful Majesty (I said), most bounteous monarch, I too petition a favor. I do not ask for gold, or precious tablets, or coverings for the altar, or high office for my kin, or a place beside your Majesty. Such things are for others, who go after trifles. I consider myself deserving of greater things. Consequently, let me have just this, permission to give way somewhat before jealousy. Let me look with reverence upon thrones, but from a distance. I am tired of being hated by everyone, even my friends, because I find myself unable to turn anywhere except to God. Enjoin in turn upon these fathers a brotherly harmony. Let them cast aside their arms out of respect for you, if not through fear of God and punishment. You, who curbed the inflexible daring of the barbarians, set up a trophy of this bloodless conflict. Demand in turn from these grey hairs (and here I indicated both them and my efforts in the cause of God) that they continue to suffer for the sake of the world. You know that it was against my will they set me on the throne."

These sentiments were publicly applauded by the emperor, and by others, too. My favor was granted, reluctantly it is true, but granted all the same. There still remained another worry in this sad affair,[82] the task of persuading everyone to accept it in good heart, and to refrain absolutely from any untoward measure they might contemplate through affection for myself and resentment of villainy. I coaxed, I praised, I tried to reconcile myself with the disaffected element, the clergy, the outsiders, the administrators of flocks, the old orthodox congregation and the recent converts who resented the loss of their pastor, and those of the bishops who were especially stricken. For there were many actually who took to flight when they

82. On vv.1905–1912 cf. A. M. Ritter, *Das Konzil*, 108.

1915 realized the project, fled from a thunderbolt as it were, covering their ears and wringing their hands, determined not to see with their own eyes another being elevated to my throne.

EPILOG, 1920–1949[83]

1920 And so the story ends. Here I am a breathing corpse,[84] vanquished (bless the mark) and garlanded. Instead of a throne and empty clamor I have God and godly friends. Taunt me then, rejoice, leap, all you wise folk, make a song of my mishaps at your meetings,[85] your parties, in your sanctuaries. Preen yourselves like conquerors for the crow of triumph. Beat your sides with your wings and arch your heads high in the concourse of fools. All of you succeeded in defeating one man who wanted to be defeated. If I wanted defeat . . . but of course in your spite you deny me even this and boast as if I were removed. But if I didn't want defeat, you are shamed by your own evil deeds, you who enthroned me yesterday and today became my persecutors.

Having extricated myself from it all, my portion shall be with the angels. As my life is now, no one shall hurt or help, I shall be all withdrawn in God. Let tongues prattle on about me like empty winds. I've had more than enough of that, people often assailed me with slanders and often with extravagant praise. I seek to live somewhere that is free from evil people, somewhere I can turn to heavenly pursuits with my spirit alone. The benign hope of things above will nourish my old age. To the churches I shall bestow my tears. Through all the vicissitudes of my life God has led me to this point. Tell me, Logos of God, whither now? Towards the unshaken seat, I pray, where is my Trinity, and that united brightness by the faint reflections of which we are now upraised.

83. G. Misch, *A History of Autobiography*, 2.616–617 reproduces the translation of H. S. Boyd, *Select Poems*, 55–56, for vv.1919–1949.
84. Cf. Sophocles, *Ant.* 1167.   85. Cf. Ps 68.13.

INDEX

INDEX

Aaron, 70, 91; Gregory the Elder as, 29 and n.
Abraham, 43 and n.; and Lot, 125 and n.; priest, 39
abyss, 63, 87, 93, 109; of filth, 64
Achaea, journey to, 35
Achaemenid Persian, 62 n.
active life, 21, 85–86
Adam, 94, 194; origin of flesh and Fall, 37
Aegina, harbor of, 83
Aeginetan craft, 83
Aelian, 55 n., 61 n.
Aeons, 109
Aeschylus, 78 n.
Aesop, 50 n.
Aetna, Mount, 116
Alexander, conquest of Seleucid kingdom by, 3
Alexandria, and Arius, 93; Christian school of, 5; church of, 12; controversy in, 11; journey from, 35; letters at, 80 and n.; mob of, 102; Peter, Patriarch of, 15; supports Paulinus, 14; voyage from, 6
Amelech, 25 and n.
Ammon, 100
Ammonites, 125
Amphilochius, 4
Anastasia, church of, 11, 17, 107 and n.
angel(s), 19, 65, 87, 109; choir of, 34, 120; Gregory's portion with, 130; moves waters of Siloe, 69; nature of, 59; nourishment of, 67; struggling, 121
Anna, holy, 39

Antioch, assembly at, 55 n.; bishop of, 119, 120; intrigues about the see of, 73 n.; Meletius of, 14; schism of, 14
Antisthenes, 105
Antony the Hermit, 6
Antonines, and endowment of chairs at Athens, 7
Anubis, 101
Apammon, 101
Apokatastasis, Origen's doctrine of, 42 n.
Apollinarian(ism), 94; controversy of, 15, 20; Gregory against, 94 and n.
Apollinarist, 51 n.
Apollo and Paul, 96 and n.
Apollonius of Rhodes, 8
apostle(s), as bishops, 55–57; inspiration of, 58; qualities of faith of, 55 and n.
Apostle John, *theologos,* 12
Aratus, 8
Arianzus, 1, 15; Gregory's retirement at, 18, 21
Argonaut expedition, 72 n.
Ares, 98 and n.
Arian(s), 10, 11, 51 n.; controversy of, 20; expulsion of by Theodosius, 13; Gregory opposes, 95 and n.; use of Aristotelian and Stoic logic of, 58 n.
Aristophanes, 52 n.
Aristotle, 8, 58 n., 61 n.; Arian use of logic of, 58 n.; and the fishing-frog, 55 n.
Arius, 6; of Alexandria, 93; and the Trinity, 93 and n.

INDEX

Ark of Noah, church as, 107 and n.
ascetic, life, 9; pioneers in Egyptian desert, 8
Assyrian, furnace, 25; yoke of, 36
Athanassiadi-Fowden, P., 6 n.
Athanasius, 6; Gregory's panegyric on, 17
Athens, 5, 6, 7, 8, 9, 11, 28; departure for, 80; departure from, 84; Gregory at, 83 and n., 84; letters at, 83 and n.; student gangs at, 83 and n.; Basil and Gregory study at, 90
Augustine, 8; *Confessions* of, 20
Aurelius, Marcus, 7
Aubineau, M., 94 n.

Babylon, rugged plains of, 36
baptism, birth through, 64; death before, 82 and n.; of Gregory, 9 and n.; Gregory's teaching on, 63 n.; purification of, 63, 65, 82; second purifying of, 64 and n.
barbarian(s), curbed by Theodosius, 129; turbulence, 112
Bareille, G., 2 n.
Basil, Saint, 51 and n.; ascetic life of, 9; death of, 10; elevation to see of Caesarea of, 9; *Epistulae*, 26, 30 n.; family of, 2, 4; funeral oration of Gregory for, 7 and n., 15, 17; meets Gregory, 5; monastic enterprise of, 9; ornament of his generation, 83–84; project for monastic life with Gregory, 8; pursues studies with Gregory, 88; religious life of at Athens, 9; *Rule of*, 10; sage of old, 87; *De spiritu sancto*, 3 n.; study of rhetoric, 5; tour of monastic sites, 9; visits at death of Caesarius, 88 and n.
Beckby, H., 19 n.
Belial, fallen from angelic state, 100; spirit the prey of, 36 and n.
Bellini, E., 1 n.
Benedictine Rule, 10
Benoît, A., 1 n.
Benrath, G. A., 20 n.
Bernardi, J., 2 n., 6 n., 16 n., 17 n., 54 n., 98 n.

bishop(s), 49, 71, 72, 107, 119, 120, 122, 129; apostles as, 55–57; bad, 50–51, 53 and n., 58; good and wise, 65, 71, 72; fashions of, 69–70; Gregory's fellow, 53; guides of precipitous routes, 78 and n.; image of, 66; leaders of the people, 77; office of, 54; requisite qualities of, 54 and n., 55; rival, 90; synod of, 51; wretched, 59–60.
blood, of innocent souls, 49; woman with issue of, 44 and n.
Boreas, 72 n.
Boulenger, F., 4 n., 5 n., 30 n.
Bowersock, G. W., 6 n.
Boyd, H. S., 81 n., 130
Browning, R., 6 n.
Byzantine, hymnology, 19; politesse, 18

Caesar, 110
Caesarea, Basil's elevation to see of, 9, 10; Christian school in Palestine, 5; in Cappadocia, 5, 89; in Palestine, 5
Caesarius, 4 and n., 9, 32, 87 and n.; decease of, 30 and n., 31, 44; estate of, 30–31; funeral oration of Gregory for, 17; in imperial palace, 31 and n.
Calais, 72 and n.
Caleb, 100
Callimachus, 8, 72 and n.
calyx, and rose, 57–58 and n.
Camelot, T., 28 n.
Capes, W. W., 7 n.
Cappadocia, 1, 2, 5; bastion of orthodoxy, 52; church of Sasima in, 89 and n.; division of, 10; southern, 3
Cappadocians, 3, 8
Carmel, 85
Carterius, 5 and n.
catechumens, 9
Catholic belief, 16
chain, golden, 28 and n.
charity, narrowness of in philosophic life, 86
chorepiscopi, 89
Christ, 2, 25, 26, 33, 44; -bearing

men, 44; call upon, 81; champion of Gregory's teaching, 96; commands of, 66; ears alien to, 110; feet of, 28; flesh of, 124; flock of, 96; grace of, 37; Gregory the Elder as friend of, 78; the King, 26, 28, 39, 42; one, 95; and the poor, 63 and n.; praising the great, 83; savior, 82; in the shadows of the Law, 109; slaying, 120; sufferings of, 52; traffickers in, 125; unerring eye of justice of, 100; will of, 39, 40; and a woman, 40.
Christian(s), 8, 9; autobiography, 20 and n., 21; belief, 2; circles, 4; convert, 12; faith, 2; families, 4; history, 2; Julian's edict excluding from teaching, 20, 55 n.; Nicaean group of, 10; parents, 8; poetic literature, 20 and n.; school, 5; studies, 80; thing to do, 52; training, 5
Christianity, 9; and family relationships, 4
Church of the Apostles, Gregory installed as patriarch of, 12; Gregory recognized by Theodosius in, 13
Chrysippus, 58 and n.
Cilicians, 3
Clement of Alexandria, 69 n.
coenobitic life, 90
colt imagery, 43, 51, 80
Coman, J., 55 n.
commandments, 110
communion, 77
conflagration, final, 49 and n.
Constantelos, D. J., 118 n.
Constantine, city of, 77
Constantinople, 2, 5, 15; assembly at, 55 n.; church of Anastasia in, 17; controversy in, 11; Council of, 12, 14, 15, 21, 118 and n., 120; Gregory called to, 51–52; legitimate bishop of, 14; patriarch of, 6; presides over Council of, 14; intrigues about the see of, 73 n.; mission of Gregory to, 11; new Rome, 93; orthodox community at, 10; Second Council of, 16; sojourn of Gregory in, 12; triumphal entry of Theodosius to, 12
contemplative life, 8, 33–35
Corinthian ladies, 103
Council of Chalcedon, 15
Council of Constantinople, 12, 14, 15, 21; Second, 16
Council of Nicaea, 14
Cox, G. V., 1 n., 3 n.
Cranz, F. E., 16 n.
Crates, 105
Cretans, 3
Crimi, C. U., 1 n.
Croesus, 62 and n.
crows, 123
Cummings, J. T., 1 n., 75 n.
cuttlefish, 110
cyathus, measuring the sea in, 58 and n.
Cynic(s), 101, 104, 105; consecration of, 102; diatribe, 53 n.; imposter, 13; Maximus, 98; philosophers, 12; philosophy of, 105; proclaimed a pastor, 103 and n.; style, 12
Cyprian, Saint, Gregory's panegyric on, 17
Cyprus, lee of, 81
Cyrus the Mede, 62 and n.

Damasus, Pope, delegate of the Council of Constantinople, 14
Daniel, 25 and n., 62 and n.
Daniélou, J., 42 n., 107 n.
Deferrari, R. J., 31 n.
Delphic priestess, 106
demons, 101
Demosthenes, 8
Dennis, G., 18 n.
Derville, A., 27 n.
Didymus the Blind, 6 and n.
Diocaesarea, 3
Diocletian, 2, 3
Diogenes, 105
Diogenes Laertius, 8, 105 n.
Dionysius, 62 n.
Diophantes, 7
disciple(s), character of, 122; Gregory as, 82; Peter as head of, 56

136   INDEX

and n.; role of, 68; storm-tossed, 25; of the Word, 96.
divine mysteries, 86
Docetism, 110
Dölger, 79 n.
Dostalova, R., 55 n.
dreams, 31, 34 and n.; of Nonna, 39 and n.

edicts of toleration, 2
Egypt, dark plain of, 36; gods of, 101, 105, 118
Egyptian(s), 6, 15; affliction by scourges of, 82 and n.; cloud, 100; contingent to Council of Constantinople, 14, 126; desert, 8; fickleness, 98; fierce, 98; fleet, 12; freak, 98; intrigue, 6; magicians, 70; plagues of, 98 and n.; Proteus, 100 and n.; rabble, 105
Eli, illustrious servant, 39 and n.
Elias the Thesbite, 66, 85.
eloquence, Gregory's, 111; road to piety, 110
Emmelia, 2
Emperor, eastern, 105; persuasion of, 113; purple-robed, 115
Engelbrecht, A., 17 n.
ephod, 69 and n.
Epiphanes, 7
episcopal, consecration, 65 n.; ministrations, 65
Ettlinger, G. H., 119 n.
Eunapius, 7
Euripus, flow of, 40 and n.
Euphranor, 72 and n.
Evagoras, 8
evangelist(s), publicans who were, 55 and n.
evil, 65, 100, 108; ignorance of, 125; innocent of, 99; steeped in, 99
exegesis, 56

Fall, 27 n.
Father, 109
fire, final, 123
fishermen and publicans, 55 and n.
fishing-frog in Aristotle, 55 and n.

Flavian, election of, 14
Fleury, E., 8 n.
Freise, R., 43 n.

Gain, B., 89 n.
Galen, 112 n.
Gallay, P., 1 n., 3 n., 4 n., 9 n., 17 n., 18 n., 80 n., 89 n.
Geanakopolos, D. J., 119 n.
Giet, S., 89 n.
God, 25, 26, 33, 34, 38, 39, 40, 41, 42, 83, 95, 116, 117; and active life, 86; almighty, 35, 38; became man, 25; beloved of, 102; books that led to, 80; chosen people of, 109; elevate a pure spirit to, 33; elevate souls to, 34; eye of, 42; fellowship with, 111 and n.; gaze directed to, 68; gift of, 39, 63; giver of light, 42; the great, 28; Gregory offered to, 79; in heaven, 31; heavenly, 29; hope of safety from, 81; image of, 40; immortal, 29; king, 34, 37; know not, 81; knowledge of, 67, 86, 109; law of, 59; laws and mysteries of, 127; means of, 80; merciful, 37; minister of, 91, 97; mysteries of, 63; offering to, 52; one, 27, 58, 63; and philosophic life, 86; privilege from, 64; propitious, 25; in psalms, 34; righteousness to, 53; salvation from, 66, 83; sent deliverance, 81; servant of, 66; sheltered by the hand of, 33; splendor of, 34; Unbegotten, 40; walk in fear of, 83; in his wisdom, 37; withdraw to, 73; Word of, 57, 126
Gorgonia, 2, 4; funeral oration of Gregory for, 17
grace, 50, 63, 64, 65, 66, 67
grammaticus, 5
Greece, 8; Athens, the glory of, 28; foundations of, 35; governor of, 7
greed, 118
Greek(s), haughty, 56; influence, 3; thought, 8; vases, 72 n.; world, 7
Gregg, R. C., 17 n.
Gregory the Elder, 86, 87, 88, 89; as Abraham, 78 and n.; baptism of,

2; Bishop of Nazianzus, 2; death of, 10 and n.; effort of to settle Gregory as auxiliary at Sasima, 91; feelings of Gregory for, 4, 28–29, 34; funeral oration of Gregory for, 17; as good shepherd, 78 n.; Gregory as coadjutor to, 10; Hypsistarian, 2; speech of as example of prosopopoiia, 91 and n.

Gregory of Nazianzus, ambitions of, 27–28; and Apollinarism, 94–95; and Arianism, 95–96; at Athens, 83–84; childhood and education, 78–80; and children, 44; choice of life, 84–86; consecration as bishop of Sasima, 89–91; and Constantinople, 93–108; and cosmetics, 98 and n.; departure for Athens, 80; departure from Athens, 84; ecclesiastical career of, 11; feelings for parents, 28–29, 34, 84, 86; and letters, 28, 85; love of sacred books, 85; and marriage, 27 and n., 40 and n., 44; ministry of, 52–53; ordination of 86–89; patriarch, 115; preaching and controversy, 108–111; recognition of by Theodosius, 12, 128–130; reputation of as orator, 11; requisite qualities of a bishop, 54 n.; resignation and retirement of, 12, 53–54, 74 and n., 126–128; return to Nazianzus, 92–93; as rhapsode, 78; as Samuel, 79 and n.; and Scripture commentaries, 56 n.; shipwreck, 80–83; speculative theology of, 11; speech of to Council of Constantinople, 14; studies with Basil, 88; and verse-making, 77; vision(s) of, 31 and n., 32, 74 and n. Works: *Ad Gregorium Nyssenum*, 89 n.; *Ad Julianum tributorum exaequatorem*, 30 n.; *Adversus Eunomianos*, 58 n., 59 n., 110 n.; *Adversus Maximum*, 103 n.; *Adversus mulieres se nimis ornantes*, 98 n.; *Apologeticus ad patrem*, 89 n.; *Apologeticus de fuga* 10, 17 and n., 87 n.; *Carmina dogmatica*, 59 n.; *Carmina moralia*, 58 n.; *Comparatio vitarum*, 19 n.; *Concerning himself and the bishops*, 21 and n.; *Concerning his own affairs*, 20–21; *Concerning his own life*, 20, 21; *Contra Julianum imperatorem*, 6 n.; *De anima*, 59 n.; *De animae suae calamitatibus carmen lugubre*, 31 n., 58 n., 74 n., 79 n.; *De filio*, 45 n., 59 n.; *De incarnatione adversus Apollinarium*, 59 n.; *De mundo*, 59 n.; *De patre*, 59 n.; *De pauperum amore*, 63 n., 111 n.; *De providentia*, 59 n.; *De rebus suis*, 50 n., 79 n., 81 n.; *De se ipso et de episcopis*, 32 n., 45 n.; *De spiritu sancto*, 29 n., 59 n., 116 n.; *De testamentis et adventu Christi*, 59 n.; *De theologia*, 58 n., 72 n., 111 n.; *De virtute*, 58 n.; *De vita sua*, 3 n., 6, 10, 12, 19 n., 20, 35 n., 53 n., 75; *Epistulae Theologicae*, 25 n.; *Epitaphia*, 4 n., 5 n., 30 n., 31 n., 58 n., 78 n., 79 n., 87 n., 91 n.; *Farewell Discourse at Constantinople*, 17; *Funebris oratio in laudem Basilii Magni Caesareae in Cappadocia episcopi*, 7 n., 62 n., 79 n., 83 n., 88 n., 111 n.; *Funebris in laudem Caesarii fratris oratio*, 4 n., 5 n., 29 n., 30 n., 31 n., 58 n., 62 n., 87 n.; *Funebris in patrem*, 2 n., 29 n., 79 n., 81 n.; funeral eulogies, 17; *In laudem Athanasii*, 29 n., 58 n., 67 n.; *In laudem Heronis philosophi*, 26 n., 103 n.; *In laudem sororis Gorgoniae*, 78 n.; *In sancta lumina*, 63 n.; *In sanctum baptisma*, 63 n.; *In sanctum Pascha et in tarditatem*, 20 n., 87 n., 88 n.; *In seipsum ad patrem et Basilium magnum*, 89 n.; *Invectives against Julian*, 17 and n.; letters, 9 and n., 15, 16, 18 and n.; *On Athanasius*, 17, 67 n., 92 n.; *On Saint Cyprian*, 17; *On his consecration to Sasima*, 17; *On Love of the Poor*, 17; *On the Maccabees*, 17; *On Moderation in Theological Discussion*, 17; *On Peace*, 17; *On the Plague of Hail*, 17; orations, 11, 16–17; poems 11, 15, 16, 19 and n.; sermons for liturgical feasts,

17; *Supremum vale*, 107 n.; *Theological Orations*, 12, 16, 17
Gregory Presbyter, 1 n.

Haggai, 65 n.
Harl, M., 56 n.
Harmon, A. M., 54 n.
Harpocras, 101
Hauser-Meury, M.-M., 1 n., 4 n., 10 n.
Heraclitus, 8
Herakles, 104
heresy, 11
heretical groups, 11
Hermanubis, 101
Hermogenes, 8
Herodotus, 8, 62 and n.
Hesiod, 8
Himerius, 8
Holy Writ, 68
Homer, 8, 26 n., 29 n., 42 n., 71 n., 98 n., 100 n., 127 n.
Homeric, style of in Gregory, 20; language and technique of in Gregory, 21
horse, 127; imagery, 62 and n., 85 and n.
Hypsistarian(s), 2 and n.
hydra, 109

Iconium, 4
imperial, decree, 105; power, 115
Incarnation, 25 n., 59, 95
Iranian, 3
Iris, river in Pontus, 9
Isaac, illustrious victim, 39
Isauria, 10
Israel, 71; chosen land of, 100; division of, 120; passage of, 82

Janin, R., 3 n.
Jericho, 37
Jerome, 8
Jerusalem, 37
Jonadab, sons of, 85 and n.
Jonas, the prophet, 127; and the whale, 25
Jones, A. H. M., 1 n., 87 n.
Joshua, 100
Jourjon, M., 17 n.

Julian, 6 and n., 9; attempt to expel Christians from schools, 20; Gregory's *Invectives Against Julian*, 17 and n.; restrictive decree of, 17, 55 n.
Jungck, C., 2 n., 19 n., 75 n.,; astronomical note on v.126, 81 n.
Junod, E., 56 n.

Keenan, M. E., 6 n.
Kennedy, G., 7 n., 30 n., 88 n.
kennelkeeper, 101, 102
Kertsch, M., 35 n.
Knecht, A., 19 n., 98 n.
Kopeček, T. A., 2 n., 54 n.
Kristeller, P. O., 16 n.
Kühn, C. G., 112 n.

Laban, and white garments, 70 and n.
Lafontaine, G., 19 n.
lamp, imagery, 15, 23, 81 and n., 94 and n.; of the Trinity, 52
Lampe, G. W. H., 2 n.
latifundia, 1
Latin, 8
Law, 109
Lazarus, 43
Leclercq, H., 3 n.
Leontius, 2
leopard, 50
Levite, 37
Libanius, 7; autobiographical oration of, 20
lion(s) 25, 50 and n., 59, 88, 96; claws of, 25; fox turns into, 62; jaws of, 25; roar of, 73
Logos of God, 24, 94
Lord, business of, 61; labor for, 53
Lorenz, B., 43 n.
Lot, and Abraham, 125 and n.
Lucian, 8, 54 n.
Lydia(n), Croesus, king of, 62 n.; chorus, 62
Lysias, 8

Maccabees, Gregory's panegyric on, 17
Macedonia(ns), 12, 15; bishops of, 14; contingent from at Council of

INDEX

Constantinople, 14, 126; Maximus in, 13; Theodosius from, 12, 112
Macrina the Elder, 2
Macrina the Younger, 2
Mani, 109
matrons, counsellor of, 62
Maximus the Cynic, 12, 13, 98 and n., 44–106
May, G., 3 n.
medicine, Byzantine, 5 and n.
Meehan, D., 18 n.
Melampus, 71 and n.
Meletius of Antioch, 119; presides over Council of Constantinople, 14; death of, 14, 120
Menander, 53 n.
Mercati, Giovanni, 18
Merra, waters of, 69
Mette, 69 n.
Michaeas, 65 and n.
Midas, 62 and n.
middle way, 86 and n.
Migne, J. P., classification of poems of Gregory in, 19; Letters of Gregory in, 18; Works of Gregory in, 16
ministry of Saint Gregory, 52–53
miracles, 114
Misch, G., 20 n., 81 n., 85 n., 130 n.
Misumenos, of Menander, 53 n.
Moabites, 125
monastic, foundations, 10; life, 8, 40; movement, 10; sites, 9
Montanus, 109
Moreschini, C., 6 n., 8 n., 17 n., 64 n.
Moses, 25 and n., 87 n.; Gregory the Elder as, 29
Mossay, J., 1 n., 16 n., 17 n., 19 n., 49 n., 98 n.
mountain and throne, 91 and n.
Mühlenberg, E., 94 n.
Mysians, 111; lands of, 69

Nathan, 70
Nautin, P., 16 n.
Nazianzus, 1, 3, 5, 9, 10, 12; church of, 10, 15, 92
Nectarius, 21; 74 and n.

New Comedy, 53 n.
New Testament, 109
Newman, J. H., 21, 83 n., 85 n.
Nicaea, Council of, 14, 127 n.; Christian group of, 10; collapsed in earthquake, 30 and n.; deliberations of, 124; doctrine of the Trinity of, 17
Nicobulus, 18 and n.
Nonna, 2, 4, 5; dream of, 79 and n.; mouth of truth, 79 and n.; ornament of women, 78 n.; prayers of, 82; promise of, 39 and n.; a second Sara, 78 and n.
Norman, A. F., 20 n.
Norris, F. W., 16 n., 58 n., 90 n.
nous, 94, 95, 110
Novatian, 109

Oberg, E., 19 n.
Old Comedy, 53 n.
Old Testament, 109
oracle(s), of Delphic priestess, 106; of Scripture, 112
Origen, 5, 10, 42 n.
orthodox(y), Cappadocia a bastion of, 52; clergy and faithful, 74 n.; communion, 77; congregation, 51, 108, 129; dissolution of, 106; doctrine, 119; Gregory as champion of, 94; Gregory criticized by, 13; in Gregory's native land, 84; group at Constantinople, 12, 13; preaching, 125; second universe of, 107; support of, 94; teaching, 108; tree of, 110; Trinitarian doctrine, 12; truth, 96; v. Arians, 11
Otis, B., 91 n.

Palatine Anthology, 4 n., 8, 19 and n., 30 n., 31 n., 78 n., 79, n., 87 n., 91 n.
Palestine, 123 n.
patria potestas, 4
Paul and Apollo, 96 and n.
Paul, Saint, 65
Paulinus, recognized by Gregory, 14; recommended by Gregory, 121 and n.; supported by Rome and Alexandria, 14

Peri, C., 19 n.
Perry, B. E., 70 n.
Persian Empire, 3
Peter, full of zeal, 56; head of the disciples, 56 and n.; as netsman, 56
Peter, leader of bishops, 101; patriarch of Alexandria, 15
Petit, P., 7 n.
Phaedrus, 70 n.
Pharaoh(s), king, 36 and n.; poisons of, 70
Philo Judaeus, 8, 52 n.
Philokalia Origenis, 10, 56 n.
philosophic life, 84, 85, 86, 89
Phocylides, 8
Phoenician merchants, 81
Phrygian(s), 111; king, 62 n.; land of, 69
Pinault, H. 6 n.
Pindar, 8
Plagnieux, J., 1 n., 27 n., 54 n.
Plato, 8 and n., 105, 112 n.; *Rep.*, 77 n., 78 n., 117 n.; style of, 58
Pliny, 60 n.
Plutarch, 8
Polycleitus, 72 and n.
Pontus, 9, 10, 87, 89
poor, 63 and n., 67; Gregory's ministry to, 111 and n., 118
preaching, 108; of Gregory, 110; orthodox character of, 125; simple, 55
Precursor, strange food of, 85
Prefect, 105
Proconesian tiles, 101 and n.
Prohairesius, 7
prophet(s), Saul among the, 61; writings of, 95, 109
prosopopoiia, vv.502–517 a good example of, 91 n.
Proteus, 71 and n.; Egyptian, 100 and n.
psalm(ody), 67, 68, 111, 118
psyche, 94, 95
Publican(s), evangelists, 55 and n.; and Pharisee, 38 and n.; Matthew as, 56 and n.
Purgatory, 49 n., 50 n.

purity and chastity, God's vision of, 31 n.
Pyrrho and Sextus, 58 and n.

Quasten, J., 1 n

Rackham, H., 60 n.
Radford-Reuther, R., 1 n.
Red Sea, 98
Regali, M., 6 n.
resurrection, 59, 108, 109, 124,
rhetor(ic), 30 n., 66; conventional, 15; and Gregory, 9, 11, 16; in Gregory's funeral oration for Basil, 7 and n.; Gregory's orations in schools of, 17; of literary genre, 4
Rhodes, 83
Rhodon, 101
Ritter, A. M., 95 n., 105 n., 112 n., 119 n., 121 n., 123 n., 126 n., 127 n., 129 n.
Roman, blood, 3; empire, 108; occupation, 3; province, 3; tradition, 4
Rome, 8; city of Constantine, 77 and n.; flourishing city of, 53; new, 93; old, 93; power of, 3; second, 119; supports Paulinus, 14
rose, and calyx, 57–58 and n.; and thorns, 90 and n.
Rousse, J., 1 n., 54 n.
Rudasso, P. R., 51 n.
Rufinus, 17 n.
Rule of St. Basil, 10

Sacred, Books, 85; Writ, 50
Sajdak, J., 103 n.
salvation, 57, 63; doctrine of, 120; from God, 60; at hands of God, 83; under God, 122; many ways of, 111; medicine of, 116
Samaritan, good, 37 and n.
Samson, 102 and n.
Samuel, Gregory as a new, 39; linen apron of, 69 and n.
Sarah, Nonna as, 39 and n.
sarx, 94
Sasima, 3 and n.; church of, 89;

INDEX

Gregory the Elder's efforts to settle Gregory there, 91; Gregory becomes bishop of, 10, 14, 89 and n., 91; see of, 9
Satan, 33; contriver of evil, 26; crooked demon, 41; demon, 26; dragon, 36; evil one, 27, 28, 31, 33, 68–69, 109; raging demon, 26; wicked demon, 98
Saul, beloved, 61 and n.
Savior, 96, 121
schism, 106, 122
Schneidewin, F. G., 70 n.
Scripture, commentaries, 56 and n.; Holy, 97, 99
sea-eagle, 60 and n.
secular, eloquence, 111; learning, 55 and n.
Seleucia, Saint Gregory flees to, 92; monastery of Saint Thecla at, 10; retreat at, 10
Seleucid Kingdom, 3
sepia fish, 41 and n.
serpent(s), hissings of, 57; offspring of, 100; rod into a, 70
Sextus and Pyrrho, 58 and n.
Shepherd, Good, 67–68, 70, 78 n.; unworthy, 68–69
shipwreck of Gregory, 80–83, 128
Sicherl, M., 19 n.
Silence, 109
Siloe, waters of, 69
Simon Magus, 62 and n.; followers of, 109
Simon Peter, 62
Simonides, 8
simony, 63 and n.
snake, 50 and n.
Socrates, 7 n., 8, 77, 105
Sodom, ashes of, 40 and n.
Son, 45 and n., 109
sophist(s), 5, 6, 8; centers of, 5; conceits of, 85; intricacies of, 80; technique of, 25 n.
Sophocles, 53 n., 69 n., 130 n.
Sozomenus, 77 n.
speakers, well-formed, candid, 57–59
Špidlík, T., 86 n.

Spirit, 101, 110; books of the, 34; bonds of the, 87; donors of the, 120; eternal, 44; explanation of, 59; grace of, 61, 94, 107; illumination of the 35 and n.; inspiration to, 57; light of, 85; mystics of, 26; overpowering influence of, 65; power of, 57; prey of Belial, 36; sacrifice of, 36; sharer in, 57; shining grace of, 34; suffused by, 56; true product of, 119
Stagirite, 58 and n.
Stippas, 101
Stoa, 105
Stoic, Arian use of logic of, 58 n.
Strabo, 3 and n.
Suidas, Lexicon, 1 n.
Sykes, D. A., 20 n.
Szymusiak-Affholder, C. M., 34 n.

Taurus, rising of, 35; tail of, 81 and n.
tax(es), booth, 54; of Caesar, 30 and n.; control of, 90; officials, 62, 89
Teja, R., 3 n.
Thasos, priest from, 101
Thecla, convent of the holy virgin at Seleucia, 92 and n.; monastery of, 10
Theocritus, 8, 33 n.
Theodosian Code, 7
Theodosius, 53 n., 103 n., 112 n.; advent of, 112–114; consents to Gregory's resignation, 14; emperor to Constantinople, 12; Maximus' appeal to, 12; pressures Gregory to attend Second Council of Constantinople, 16; recognition of Gregory by, 12, 13
Theognis, 8
theologus, epithet of Gregory, 12
Thespesius, 5
Thessalonica, base of Emperor, 105 and n.
Thompson, D'Arcy W., 61 n.
thorns, 112; and roses, 90 and n.; of living, 26; thicket of, 38
Thracians, 53 and n.
Thrason, in New Comedy, 53 n.

Thrasonides, 53 n.
throne(s), 53, 61, 63, 64, 66, 68, 73, 77, 89, 97, 105, 113, 127; elevation of Gregory to, 87; episcopal, 115, 119; and mountain, 91 and n.; rivalry about, 120
Thucydides, 8
Tiberius, 3
Tillemont, 1 n.
Timothy, epistle to, 65 n.
Trajan, 3
tribon, 7
Trinitarian doctrine, 12
Trinity, 58, 96, 106, 107, 122, 128, 130; incorruptible, 109; lamp of, 52; light of, 31; preaching of, 108; sacred nature of, 124; and Theodosius, 113
Trisoglio, F., 1 n., 7 n., 20 n.
trumpet(s), 82 and n.
Tuilier, A., 19 n.
two ways, 26 and n.
tyranny, 87 and n.

Ullman, C., 1 n., 3 n.

Valens, 3; death of, 10; division of Cappadocia by, 10

Vergil, 42 n., 127 n.
Vespasian, 3
virgin(s), 103; counsellor of, 62; Gregory's ministry and, 118; son of, 95

Waltz, P., 19 n.
wasps, 123
Way, A. C., 16 n.
Weeger, J., 27 n.
Werhahn, H. M., 19 n., 111 n.
whale, 96
wickedness, 104
Winslow, D. F., 1 n., 8 n., 63 n., 73 n.
wolf(ves), 50, 97, 102, 107; in the midst of, 52
Word, 94, 95; contemplation of, 85; Gregory a disciple of, 96; of God, 57, 126; saving, 43; subjection to, 28 and n.; one wise, 90
Wyss, B., 1 n., 2 n., 8 n., 18 n., 20 n., 29 n., 53 n., 55 n., 58 n., 69 n.

Zachaeus, 63 and n.
Zetes, 72 n.
Zeuxis, 72 and n.

www.ingramcontent.com/pod-product-compliance
Lightning Source LLC
Chambersburg PA
CBHW032041290426
44110CB00012B/894